D1480062

$19.95

364.1523 Chen, Edwin,
CHE 10/96 Deadly
scholarship : the

THE BRUMBACK LIBRARY

OF VAN WERT COUNTY
VAN WERT, OHIO

GAYLORD

Deadly Scholarship

DEADLY SCHOLARSHIP

The True Story of Lu Gang
and Mass Murder
in America's Heartland

Edwin Chen

A Birch Lane Press Book
Published by Carol Publishing Group

364.1523
CHE

Copyright © 1995 by Edwin Chen

All rights reserved. No part of this book may be reproduced in any form, except by a newspaper or magazine reviewer who wishes to quote brief passages in connection with a review.

A Birch Lane Press Book
Published by Carol Publishing Group
Birch Lane Press is a registered trademark of Carol Communications, Inc.
Editorial Offices: 600 Madison Avenue, New York, N.Y. 10022
Sales and Distribution Offices: 120 Enterprise Avenue, Secaucus, N.J. 07094
In Canada: Canadian Manda Group, P.O. Box 920, Station U, Toronto, Ontario M8Z 5P9
Queries regarding rights and permissions should be addressed to Carol Publishing Group, 600 Madison Avenue, New York, N.Y. 10022

Carol Publishing Group books are available at special discounts for bulk purchases, sales promotions, fund-raising, or educational purposes. Special editions can be created to specifications. For details, contact Special Sales Department, Carol Publishing Group, 120 Enterprise Avenue, Secaucus, N.J. 07094

Manufactured in the United States of America

10 9 8 7 6 5 4 3 2 1

Library of Congress Cataloging-in-Publication Data

Chen, Edwin
   Deadly scholarship : the true story of Lu Gang and mass murder in America's heartland / by Edwin Chen.
      p.   cm.
   A "Birch Lane Press book."
   ISBN 1-55972-241-X (cloth)
   1. Lu Gang, d. 1991.   2. Murders—Iowa—Biography.
3. University of Iowa—Students—Biography.   4. Mass murder—Iowa—Case studies.   I. Title.
HV6248.L84C54
364.1'523'09777655—dc20   94-190441
                                                                CIP

To Matthew Chen

Contents

(Illustrations follow pages 44 and 76.)

Foreword

When I learned about the November 1, 1991, mass murders at the University of Iowa, my interest was instantly piqued.

Even in so generally violent a society as ours, multiple killings in any small Midwestern town do not happen every day. Mass murders on a serene Iowa college campus? Rarer still.

The gunman turned out to be a freshly minted Ph.D. in astrophysics—one of the best ever seen at the university, an institution with a long and worldwide reputation as a hotbed for space scientists. In fact, the building that houses the Department of Physics and Astronomy, where four of the killings occurred, is named for James Van Allen, the native Iowan who discovered the deadly radiation belts that gird planet Earth. They, too, bear his name.

Three of the murder victims were faculty members at the department, including its chairman, and were leading theoreticians in the field. A fourth victim, the killer's primary target, was a former roommate-turned-archrival, also a "post-doc" in physics—but an even more celebrated student and researcher. The fifth person killed that day was a popular university associate vice president whose duties included the handling of student grievances, such as those harbored by the killer.

As a Washington-based science policy reporter, I was immediately fascinated by the larger forces that gave added context to the horrendous crimes: the intense pressures and vicious competition that increasingly beset academic scientists throughout America.

By the mid-1980s, the explosive growth in the number of university-based researchers began to outpace the public's ability to support their work, leading inevitably to an ever-tightening job market. All over the country, grant proposals for meritorious research projects were being turned down, often summarily. Even established, award-winning scientists could no longer count on continued research support. Rather, getting ahead now seemed to depend more on back-channel connections, and on one's flair for self-promotion, than on either pure ingenuity at the bench or the power of original thought.

Furthermore, despite the growing alarm and dismay that permeated the ranks of academic (and even industrial) researchers, prospects for better days seemed nowhere near the horizon. In the marbled halls of Congress, scientists became a familiar—if awkward—sight, shuffling from one member's office to another like so many Washington lobbyists, pleading for special consideration. This sorry sight was due in no small part to Washington's profligate deficit-spending policies during the Reagan and Bush years.

By the time Bill Clinton became President, the United States had fallen behind Japan and Germany in nondefense spending for research and development as a percentage of the gross domestic product. Also, public disenchantment with the scientific community was growing, fueled by spectacularly questionable conduct—such as the now-discredited cold fusion experiments at the University of Utah, and the gross misuse of public funds by Stanford University. Additionally, at the University of California in San Diego, Ian Kennedy left in disgrace after he was exposed for having performed cloning experiments using a prohibited virus, in flagrant disregard of government safety standards. And at Rutgers University in New Jersey, a

tenured professor was fired for having used foreign graduate students to do landscaping and paint his house. And so
it went, here and there, now and again.

Although in toto such abuses may be rare, all too
prevalent indeed is academia's systematic exploitation of
graduate students that forces them to compete in a dog-eat-
dog world, working day and night for a pittance, striving to
get ahead in fields already suffering from a glut of unemployed Ph.D.s. For the foreign students who also must cope
with cultural and linguistic barriers, often with little or no
assistance from either their host universities or the local
communities, such pressures are daunting, to say the least.

Yet professional and social pressures are hardly limited to academia. And such competition commonly does
not drive people to commit violence against fellow human
beings. Clearly there were other demons at work to explain
the rampage at the University of Iowa.

I became more intrigued still upon learning that both
the killer and his primary target were scholars from the
People's Republic of China—two of the best physics students ever to come out of that country. One, Lu Gang, was
from Beijing, the only son of a doctor and a clerk. His
victim, Shan Linhua, was the eldest son of dirt-poor tenant
farmers in a remote village.

As I began delving into the complex factors that led to
this mass murder on the college campus, I found myself
becoming increasingly curious about the education-ori-
ented programs, conditions, and circumstances that existed during the turbulent times when my own parents
came to America. Like thousands of their peers, they left a
war-torn China in the 1940s, bravely risking a journey
across the Pacific for the chance to study in the United
States—a country that the Chinese lyrically call "Meiguo,"
or Beautiful Nation.

What was it like, for the thousands of China's elite able
to escape from their own deteriorating educational sys-

tems, to study here? What became of them? And what about all those who had come long before them—long before China was torn asunder, first by the Japanese and then by the Chinese themselves?

In more modern times, how did the rocky relations between Washington and Beijing affect that flow? How were the Chinese treated? Were they exploited, either by unscrupulous individuals or by the system at large? How well did they assimilate? What did they contribute? What did they take back home with them—if they returned at all? And to what extent did fear of retribution after the Tiananmen Square Massacre in 1989 exert new pressures on the Chinese students here to find ways, legal and otherwise, to delay or avoid going home?

Deadly Scholarship is the result of my search for answers to these (and many other) questions that arose after the angry shots were fired on that bleak Friday afternoon of November 1, 1991, shattering the innocence of a bucolic Big Ten college campus sequestered in America's heartland.

Acknowledgments

Many people helped make this book possible.

At the *Los Angeles Times*, the support of Editor C. Shelby Coffey III, National Editor Mike Miller, Washington Bureau Chief Jack Nelson, and Deputy Washington Bureau Chief Richard T. Cooper cleared the way. Assignment Editor Diane Spatz was once again graciously accommodating.

In Iowa City, so many people helped me in so many different ways that I cannot possibly enumerate each act of kindness or friendship. But I would like to especially thank Mike and Betsy Altmaier, Erik Nilausen, and Cheryl Tugwell. Similarly, James A. Van Allen was unfailingly cooperative, taking time out repeatedly from his busy schedule to provide me with information, assistance, and insights.

I also would like to thank University of Iowa journalism professor Judy Polumbaum for her permission to borrow from her insightful article in the November 1992 issue of *Iowa City* magazine. Her piece, "Shan Linhua: The Forgotten Victim," provided illuminating new details. Permission to quote from Polumbaum's piece also was granted by *Iowa City* publisher Christopher Green.

Another pioneering piece of work was done by a *Los Angeles Times* Washington Bureau colleague, Jim Mann, who was the first to interview Lu Huimin.

My work was made immensely easier because of the timely assistance of four topflight researchers: Lisa Buckley, Monica M. Downer, John Kenyon, and Lisa Schafer.

Downer began her research for me in Iowa, and continued it in China.

Many people with whom I met cited various reasons for requesting anonymity. But their contributions were no less important, because they had direct knowledge of important events. Where these people are cited in the book, then, their suggested initials are used to honor their desire not to be fully identified.

I would like to thank Donald Alton, Joan Alton, Gary Althen, An Tao, Ken Balis, Laura Behrens, Alan R. Bohanan, Margaret B. Brooke, William B. Casey, Rev. Jason Chen, Chi Xuming, Paul D. Cleary, Jeanne Marie Duvall, Wilma Fairbank, Fan Fan, John D. Fix, William Fuhrmeister, Gary W. Galluzzo, Jim Grutzmacher, Donald A. Gurnett, Judi Gust, Paul J. Hansen, Tom Jorgenson, Linda Kettner, Craig Lihs, Liu Chuan, John G. Lyons, Robert A. McCown, Julia Mears, Roger Mildenstein, Rev. Tom Miller, Peter E. Nathan, Pat Needle, Jane M. Nicolson, Gerald L. Payne, Karen Phelps, Wayne N. Polyzou, Hunter R. Rawlings III, Ann M. Rhodes, Evelyn Robison, William R. Robison, John Rogers, Bill Schafer, Shan Huang, Vanessa Shelton, Leslie B. Sims, Miya Rodolfo-Sioson, David J. Skorton, Kathlin Smith, Robert Smith, Brookes Spector, Marjorie Stanton, Kenneth Starck, Donald H. Strand, William Theisen, Abigail Halsey Van Allen, J. Patrick White, Janet White, Stanley White, W. J. Winkelhake, and Yang Yiling.

Also extremely helpful and courteous were the staffs of the Committee on Scholarly Communications With China, the National Association of Foreign Student Affairs, the Iowa City Historical Society, the Iowa City Chamber of Commerce, and the University of Iowa archives, special collections.

Several more people deserve special mention.

I must cite first Barbara Lowenstein, my agent. Her perseverance and perspicacity were what, from scratch, both inspired and enabled me to create this book as you now see it.

The advice and counsel of Eileen Schlesinger Cotton, my editor—who inherited the project in midstream but treated it as her own—was a godsend. Also immensely helpful were the suggestions of James Ellison, who played an essential and much-appreciated role in shaping the final product.

Nancy T. Chen, my mother, voluntarily translated endless pages of material for me.

Meredith Ferguson Chen, my wife and a widely published writer herself, provided insightful research and made numerous incisive observations all along the way.

Finally, Matt Chen would be disappointed if I didn't mention Zellie Rose Chen, a steady companion throughout the project.

Author's Note

Most U.S. news accounts of the murders at the University of Iowa referred to the killer as Gang Lu and to his archrival as Linhua Shan. Indeed many people on campus referred to them that way. But throughout this book, I have adopted the Chinese usage, in which the surnames (Lu and Shan) precede the given names. Other Chinese students are referred to in the same manner.

Readers may wonder about the cases of, say, Jean Jew or T. D. Lee. Because they are both Chinese-Americans, rather than Chinese nationals, I have employed the Western usage.

A final word about the identification of some sources. A number of people whom I interviewed asked to remain anonymous, for a variety of reasons. Where they are identified at all, I have assigned them random initials.

Deadly Scholarship

Prologue

They both were brilliant scholars. Each was ranked by most of the veteran faculty members as among the very best ever to do graduate work in physics at the University of Iowa. Both came from China. But there the similarities ended.

Shan Linhua was the humble son of impoverished peasants from the countryside. Lu Gang was the haughty son of government workers from the capital of Beijing.

Shan was lean, and possessed a certain physical grace that bespoke athletic prowess. Lu was uncoordinated, and a tad flabby under the loose-fitting shirts he liked to wear.

Shan, who spoke fluent English and was utterly self-possessed, was quick to flash an infectious grin. Almost from the day that he arrived in Iowa City, he developed a wide circle of friends and admirers.

Lu was distant, struggling with English and plagued by social awkwardness. Despite his dogged efforts to assimilate, he remained a pathetic loner, more likely to sulk than to smile.

"Shan had an outgoing personality. He was difficult *not* to get to know," recalled Karen Phelps, the physics department's administrative assistant who knew both doctoral candidates. "He sang in the hallways, and always said hello to people as they went by."

Lu, on the other hand, kept pretty much to himself, generally speaking only when spoken to, and preferring to look down or away when passing a fellow student in the

long, narrow corridors of Van Allen Hall. Whereas casual
observers often assumed he was lost in thought over some
research problem, Lu more often than not was raging over
some slight—real or (more often than not) imagined.

Half a world away from home, fate cast Shan and Lu
together as contenders in a major educational arena. And
for years, largely side-by-side, they studied, competed,
performed astrophysics research, and occasionally even
socialized. For nine months, they even shared an off-
campus apartment—Shan to save money for his wedding,
Lu to better keep an eye on an emerging rival who
increasingly posed a threat to his status in the Department
of Physics and Astronomy.

ONE

Distant Scholar

They met on a warm, lazy day in early autumn, when the academic year was still fresh and full of promise. Although it was too early for the leaves to begin changing colors, by late afternoon the September sun was already starting to cast long, dancing shadows across the bustling campus of the China University of Science and Technology.

He spotted her as she was walking home after class, and decided that it was at last time to make her acquaintance. For quite some time Shan Linhua had often noticed this pretty coed in particular, for she seemed to spend more time on campus than most other students. And soon Shan discovered the reason: She lived *on* campus, in an apartment provided her family by the university—because her father was a professor of engineering there.

Until now, however, Shan had never quite made the overture; he was almost totally preoccupied with physics and space science. Finally in his senior year at the prestigious university, one of China's top science institutions, Shan had high hopes of going abroad in the following year, to study for a doctoral degree. And his dream was to do that in the United States. All he had to do was score near the top on the rigorous national qualifying examinations.

Yang Yiling also was in her final year at the university, completing a degree in electrical engineering. And for some time now she had noticed Shan as well. Indeed, it would have been hard to miss this handsome, athletic-looking young man with the engaging smile and hordes of friends. This elite university, after all, was not all that large. With less than 3,400 undergraduates and 150 graduate students, the campus actually had somewhat of a cozy atmosphere—a rare academic refuge in a teeming nation of more than 1.2 billion people.

The pressures at the university were intense, though that didn't stop legions of students (especially on Friday afternoons) from putting aside their books to let off some steam by joining in spirited games of soccer or basketball. But even in such blur-of-activity groups Shan stood out—and the watchful Yang often spotted him easily as she trudged toward the library.

Shan played with relish and infectious abandon, his well-toned physique glistening with perspiration as he loped gracefully up and down the grassy soccer field or the basketball court. When game-oriented disputes arose, it was Shan who arbitrated, settling things in a way that made everyone laugh. During water breaks, he was the person around whom the others tended to gather. He was the kind of person who made things *happen*—and she liked that.

Yang didn't learn until later that Shan was also one of the most brilliant physics students in all of China. But she might have guessed—because it wasn't unusual for Yang to look up from her studies in the library and see him, just hours after watching him hard at play.

And so, on that idyllic fall afternoon in 1985, Yang was pleasantly surprised to see Shan angling toward her, cutting across the grassy yard with a determined yet friendly look. Finally, she thought to herself. After all this time.

"Do you want to talk to me?" Shan asked, smiling, as their eyes locked.

"Yes," Yang answered with a demure smile of her own as she quickly cast her dark eyes slightly downward.

The attraction was mutual and immediate—and thus began a whirlwind courtship.

At that first meeting, Shan told Yang that he was the son of uneducated tenant farmers who eked out a living in their ancestral village, a tiny and remote community of some five hundred hardy souls to the south of the university. Yang was surprised to learn that this urbane and obviously very intelligent young man was the product of China's countryside, where schools had always been inferior and were still struggling to recover from the disastrous Cultural Revolution of 1966–1968.

A slender woman with thick, shiny black hair that fell over her shoulders, and a shy but engaging—almost innocently playful—smile, Yang had never met anyone from such a distinctly peasant upbringing. His parents, Jiarong and Zhuwen, were semi-illiterate. But that was hardly surprising. As many as 80 percent of China's peasants still could not read.

Their backgrounds could hardly have been more different. Yang's father was a university professor; her mother was a medical doctor. Yang was born in the southern metropolis of Nanjing, where she had spent her first fifteen years. Her family moved to Hefei when her father took a job at the China University of Science and Technology in Anhui province.

But now, as graduating seniors, Shan and Yang had much elsewise in common. And she found herself captivated by his surmounting of his humble origins. Clearly, Shan had already successfully transformed himself by dint of his intellect. His future seemed limitless.

The first of three boys born to peasant farmers who

were still tilling the land, Shan spent his youth unquestioningly harvesting two rice crops a year, in a ritual older than China herself. The family lived in a two-room house made of brick, mud, and wood, as did most of China's 430 million farm families.

The Shans felt blessed to have three strong sons to help them work the land. In succession, at a tender age Shan and his brothers began pitching in, tending to the pigs and chickens, and twice a year working alongside their parents, planting rice seedlings. All three boys would end up, like their parents, with scarred fingertips as a result of knife accidents while chopping grass to feed their sheep.

Though they harbored few ambitions for themselves, Shan's parents inculcated in the boys the need to study hard. And they all took that advice to heart—especially Shan. Almost from the start, he seemed destined to become a shining product of what is by far the world's largest education system.

With 1.1. million regular schools, China has nearly 10 million teachers, and more than 200 million full-time students. And there also are more than 227,000 special adult-education schools with 355,000 teachers and 25.8 million students. But the system is also extremely competitive. Of the 202.6 million students, only 7 million graduate from senior middle school, with just 2 million going on to college. And of the annual 500,000 college graduates, only 45,000 pursue graduate studies. Shan was one of those who made it to the top.

At the village schoolhouse, Shan proved to be a fast learner and was a topflight student throughout his eight years in the primary grades. At home in the evenings, after finishing his farm chores, he often wandered down the street to visit a distant relative, Ni Daxing, who was a physics teacher and principal at the township junior middle school. If Shan was seeking to adopt the educator as a scholastic mentor, dropping by several nights a week with questions about math and science, Ni was only too happy to comply. For the old man was impressed by this precocious child with a driving desire to master his school subjects. Indeed, in more than twenty years of teaching peasant children, Ni had never seen one with quite the special qualities that this young man possessed. He was convinced that Shan would go far in life.

As Shan was finishing up at the village school, his father feared that even his brightest son might not get into college, despite the top grades. And so he urged Shan to consider enrolling in a vocational school, which would at least teach him some practical skills. But Ni Daxing wouldn't hear of it. He persuaded Shan's father to let the boy take the qualifying examinations for senior middle school—the academic track leading toward college. Sure enough, Shan excelled on the tests, and in the autumn of 1979 left to attend a senior middle school in Jiaxing, a sooty, undistinguished industrial city of 150,000 in the southern province of Zhejiang.

Behind the walls of the Number One Middle School in Jiaxing, Shan lived, played, and most of all immersed himself in the study of both the natural sciences and the liberal arts. There, he was surrounded by other peasant children whose outstanding accomplishments also had given them a shot at avoiding a drab lifetime of subsistence farming, vying instead for a place in the highest ranks of China's elite. It was also there that Shan began to learn English.

Nobody studied harder or pushed himself more, and Shan's grades showed it. His marks were nearly always the best in his class. But Shan also was appreciated by his teachers as a modest, unassuming student who was quick to help others. "He was very studious," said Yang Peichu, his chemistry teacher, in an interview with *Iowa City* magazine. "And yet he was down-to-earth. He was also very good to others. He was like a mini-teacher in the class.

Students with questions often went to him for help. He usually didn't have problems; he could solve his own problems. He liked to figure things out on his own."

At the school, Shan shared a small and dimly lit dormitory room with seven other boys. They slept in rickety wooden bunk beds shoved close together. Shan often returned home during school vacations and for monthly visits, which meant riding a bus for more than an hour and then walking for another sixty minutes. But he rarely passed up the opportunity to go home: There was always farm work to be done, and his family could use an extra pair of hands—even if no longer calloused.

After two years at the Number One Middle School, there was no longer any doubt that Shan was on a trajectory toward the highest ranks of China's intellectual class. Still, when he sat down to take the National College Entrance Examinations in the summer of 1981, he faced long odds: It was as a rule extremely difficult for students from the interior to compete successfully for slots in China's universities and colleges. Given the inferior quality of the schools in the countryside, the obstacles often proved insurmountable. All one had to do was look at the students already in the best universities; the overwhelming majority were from urban areas.

Yet Shan did extremely well in every subject. In physics, he scored a perfect 100—a virtually unheard-of feat. That gained him admission to the China University of Science and Technology, one of several institutions in that country described as "China's MIT."

Impressive by any standard, Shan's climb was all the more remarkable in a country where one's origins and family circumstances more often than not dictated social status and educational opportunities. And this was especially true for peasants, who made up 80 percent of China's population. But—in addition to his own brilliance and drive—Shan also benefited from lucky timing.

The central government was stressing the importance of science and technology precisely when he was ready for college. And outstanding students, regardless of status or family origin, found themselves facing an unprecedented array of opportunities, including the possibility of studying abroad. Another break came in 1985—the year in which Shan competed for a slot to study physics in the United States: Beijing announced that it would increase by one-third the number of state-financed students going abroad to study. A foreign education for its students had not always been high on China's list of priorities, but, facing an increasingly competitive global market, it was now desperate to make up for lost time.

To be sure, China's veneration of scholarship goes back thousands of years, with ancient scholar-officials enjoying great respect and status. As early as the eighth century, Tang dynasty rulers devised for bureaucrats a rigorous system of examinations to replace those that had been allowed to decay by previous emperors. To prepare for the government-administered examinations usually required years of classical studies and a mastery of poetry, philosophy, and literature that only the wealthiest could afford. Yet the system also won broad support from the lower classes, since it enabled anyone who studied diligently and passed the exacting examinations to also acquire wealth and power—perhaps even becoming a minister in the emperor's court. Thus the Tang rulers had created the beginnings of a true civil-service merit system that would become one of the greatest achievements of Chinese civilization.

Although at first there was little emphasis on the sciences, engineering, technology, and foreign languages, over the centuries it began to dawn on the imperial court that China was increasingly at a competitive disadvantage against Western nations that put far greater emphasis on technical expertise. And eventually—by the nineteenth century—China would create numerous "modern" schools (many with ties to foreign missionaries) in order to prepare fresh generations of the ruling class skilled in foreign languages, sciences, technology, and engineering.

Initially such schools had to overcome a second-class image. They were disdained by the traditionalists because their graduates were poorly prepared for the civil-service examinations—still the time-honored route to prestigious government careers. To a large extent, of course, the classically trained officials felt threatened by the emerging class of technocrats, who by definition did not share the common ethos of preserving the traditional, political, and economic status quo. Such tensions lingered into the twentieth century.

Beijing finally eliminated the traditional civil-service examinations in 1905 and created a Ministry of Education. The abolition of the examination system was a final triumph for the technocrats. Now the "modern" schools— and a mastery of practical skills and Western know-how— became the fast track to personal advancement and national self-strengthening efforts alike.

But China's overhaul of her educational system during the first half of the twentieth century was hardly a steady march. It was severely disrupted first by the Japanese invasion, and then by the civil war between Mao Tse-tung's Communists and Chiang Kaishek's Nationalists. Despite the upheaval, as many as 200 colleges and universities strove mightily to maintain a broad curriculum, particularly in technical training. But the best and brightest students were sent abroad for advanced degrees. And most of these 40,000 young people returned as professionals who were quickly given important jobs in government.

At the same time, the emphasis on science and technology filtered down to the secondary schools, with special attention paid to early specialization.

After Mao took power with the founding of the People's Republic of China on October 1, 1949, the Communists set out to further modernize the country's education system— and to make it more egalitarian. By 1952, China had adopted the Soviet Union's model, which emphasized science and technology, institutional specialization, and centralized control by the government. Primary and secondary schools were revamped. New facilities were built, old ones were rehabilitated; enrollments were increased; new teachers were trained; fresh materials, translated from Russian, were provided. Many "key" schools were created in order to attract the best teachers and students.

"Study hard, serve the country, and get ahead," became the era's credo. Education and expertise were highly valued, and those who embarked on a specialized path could look forward to a stable and rewarding career.

Or so it seemed.

In 1958, Mao mobilized the nation to meet a developing economic crisis—a move that quickly brought shattering consequences for education. A peasant himself, Mao had become increasingly perturbed by the deep chasm between rural and urban China. In the cities, arrogant bureaucrats and aloof intellectuals had become wedded to a privileged life of power, wealth, and creature comforts.

In Beijing, the state-and-party apparatus had achieved effective, centralized control over the nation's economy, but agricultural production was stagnating. Urban population was growing rapidly, while government grain collections hardly increased at all, due in part to the spread of red tape and corruption.

To remedy the situation and stimulate both the industrial and agricultural sectors, Mao declared a Great Leap Forward. In effect, he was abandoning the Soviet model of taxing agriculture to build industry. It just wasn't working.

And so millions of city-dwellers, against their will, were dispatched to the countryside, to join the masses mobilized to help build irrigation ditches, flood-control channels, and assorted land-reclamation projects. Decentralized planning and management became the watchwords. And, largely by dint of sheer muscle power, tens of thousands of reservoirs and power plants were built, as were countless canals, highways, and bridges.

With much fanfare, communes with as many as 70,000 peasants were formed in the villages by merging agricultural production cooperatives. These communes also performed various local government functions—all under the control of the Chinese Communist Party. No one could own chickens or pigs. Private plots were seized. Production brigades were formed. Women joined men in the fields. Teams were assigned to farm collectively, using commonly owned tools.

Tedious political meetings were held, during which people with advanced education and expertise were severely criticized for engaging in selfish "careerism." But in the end, Mao's utopian vision of grand, agricultural "cities" with proletarianized peasants as residents was doomed. "This revolution collapsed from general overwork and exhaustion," said Harvard University's John K. Fairbank, the late dean of China scholars.

The demise of the revolution was hastened by harsh weather that devastated harvests in huge portions of China, and by the withdrawal of Soviet technicians and financial aid. Gross national product dropped by as much as one-third. Transportation broke down. Malnutrition spread. By 1959, the Great Leap Forward was dead, and China had resumed its policy of promoting education and the development and specialization of expertise.

By the time Shan Linhua was born, in 1964, China was well on her way to having a modern, egalitarian educational system able to produce legions of newly educated young people prepared to belatedly help bring China into the twentieth century. In fact, from 1950 to 1966 nearly half of all college students were majoring in science and engineering. And tens of thousands more were studying abroad, mostly in the Soviet Union and Eastern Europe.

Then, starting in 1966, China once more was torn asunder. With the tumultuous Great Proletarian Cultural Revolution, Mao attempted to wipe out the ancient ruling-class tradition and create, according to Fairbank, "a propertyless class culture." During what became a decade-long interregnum, when the rule of law broke down and chaos reigned, no part of the Chinese social wherewithal was more severely disrupted than education. To an even greater extent than during the Great Leap Forward, expertise was scorned and professionals were persecuted. Scholars and specialists—often in their prime of life—were forced to abandon their professions, and were banished to camps in the countryside, to perform hard labor and undergo "reeducation."

This anti-intellectual fervor swept all of China, shutting down colleges and universities. Initially, most primary and secondary schools also were closed down. But many reopened within a few months, with sharply higher enrollments than before. In the spirit of class struggle, the school doors were flung open to all. The quality of instruction plummeted, though, since most of the best teachers—like their collegiate counterparts—had been dispatched to the countryside.

In launching the Cultural Revolution, Mao had grown to abhor what he saw as the decadent city life. In his own mind, the ideal Chinese was the all-around peasant farmer who, when necessary, became a militia soldier—as millions had during the Chinese Civil War. Education and economics had to take a back seat to political correctness. The peasants, in short, needed to rise up against the professional, trained, urban elite.

And so traditional textbooks were banned from the schools. In village elementary schools, "barefoot doctors" were trained to work among the common people in the countryside. Urban functionaries were dispatched to the fields to perform manual labor.

By 1971 some colleges and universities were allowed to reopen, but their curricula were halved, and filled with political indoctrination, manual labor, and production-oriented training. They were lacking in both foreign-language training and the basic sciences. The students were selected not on merit, but handpicked by their "production units" on the basis of such political considerations as one's "class background." In short, education was effectively reduced to the lowest common denominator.

By 1976, however, Mao was dead—and with him the Cultural Revolution, leaving in their broad and choppy wake a "lost generation" of more than 100 million floundering and foundering young people.

Moving quickly to repair its devastated educational system, China restored intellectuals to positions of influence and began to train new specialists. Academic achievement and aptitude were reinstated as the primary criteria for admission to the best middle schools as well as to colleges and universities. Whereas only 20 percent of China's school-age children had actually been enrolled in 1949, 95 percent were in school by the time Shan Linhua had graduated from kindergarten. During this time, as many as 150 million adults also learned to read.

Renewed emphasis now was placed on agriculture, industry, national defense, and science and technology—the so-called four modernizations. By the thousands, the best students once again were sent abroad for advanced training. And the dire need to nurture and train young students who could help narrow the widening gap between China and the rest of the world was not lost on older professionals like Ni Daxing, the aging village tutor.

All over China, middle schools, including Ni's, began to offer a wide variety of elective courses, ranging from map-making and literature to foreign languages and basic astronomy. By the time Shan became a student at the Number One Middle School in Jiaxing in the early 1980s, the school was offering after-hours lectures on computer sciences, fiber optics, lasers, bioengineering, and much, much more. Such exposure further paved the way for Shan to make a smooth transition to college.

At the university level, one of the beneficiaries of this new era was the China University of Science and Technology, which rose from the ashes of the Great Leap Forward. Now known as one of China's foremost centers of science and technology, the university has four research institutes, thirty-eight laboratories, and nine academic departments—including physics. It also publishes its own journal. In the 1980s, its vice president was the physicist Fang Lizhi, one of Shan Linhua's professors, whose human-rights advocacy led to his banishment from China.

After leaving for the Number One Middle School in Jiaxing, Shan never lived at home again for any extended time—but he never forgot those he left behind. From Hefei he wrote to Bian Qucheng, his English instructor at the Number One Middle School in Jiaxing, about university life: "The competition is fierce, and the level of hardship even fiercer than in the exams for senior middle school. As I look back upon the path I have traveled, of course I must thank my college teachers. They gave me the chance. And I thank my middle school teachers even more. It's you who gave me the foundation. In my success is your blood and sweat. Let us share in our happiness."

At the China Institute of Science and Technology, Shan had found true joy. And now, on a fading autumn afternoon in 1985, as he and Yang Yiling strolled aimlessly about the 840-acre university campus, textbooks in hand, Shan said he would be going to Beijing in the following month, to take yet another grueling battery of examinations. This time, he was seeking to win a coveted spot in a highly competitive, government-sponsored program that each year sent about 100 of China's top physics graduates to the United States, to work on their doctoral degrees. Even though she had never heard of the program, Yang was impressed—and she made a mental note to ask around about it.

Privacy and space being scarce in most of China, Shan and Yang spent much of their time together strolling in parks, and occasionally seeing a movie. From the start, Yang was impressed by his genuine interest in her and her family. He of course talked about himself and his background, but never, she felt, in a self-centered or boastful way. Rather, he seemed eager that she get to know him much better much faster.

If Shan seemed a bit too much in a hurry to push things between them, Yang told herself, it was probably because he was so aware that he might be leaving the country soon after graduation. Thus it was that, as the happy days and weeks passed, the prospect of Shan's going abroad began to loom large in Yang's mind as well. Perhaps like so many other Chinese scholars who went to the United States on study programs, he would never return. At one point, she even toyed with the idea of *not* pursuing their blossoming friendship. "I thought he'd find a pretty American girl," she told more than one close friend.

Try as she might, however, Yang was unable to hold in check her deepening affection for this self-possessed young man who showed no traces of his peasant origins. Her spirits soared further still after Shan returned from his two-week trip to Beijing in October. With Yang again and strolling in the park, Shan told her that he had missed her very, very much. Yang shyly confessed that she had sorely missed him, too. From that moment on, their fate was joined.

Though Yang, the eldest of three siblings, was strong-willed, she felt at ease in letting Shan take the initiative during their courtship. By January, around the time of the Spring Festival, he suggested that it was time he met her parents. "I think they'll like me," he said.

Yang's parents frankly had doubts about the budding romance. They felt that their daughter, at age twenty-one, might well be too young to be so serious about a man. "But we'd like to meet him," said her mother. (They had never seen their daughter so happy.) Not surprisingly, Shan quickly won them over. He clearly cared deeply for Yang, and was lovingly solicitous toward her—in an understated way that was not put on for their benefit.

Yang's parents also were impressed with Shan Linhua's maturity, for he possessed a poise far beyond his twenty-one years and his peasant-stock background. Without being egotistical, he was very much at ease with himself—a friendly, outgoing scholar with a well-rounded personality who knew that he was destined for high achievement. Yet he did not let his ambitions obscure his practical outlook: "Study English," he urged Yang. "It's the language of the future."

With spring arrived Shan's notification that he had placed sixty-second out of more than 1,000 graduating seniors in physics who took the qualifying examinations to study in the United States. In the fall he would be heading for America—his first trip ever abroad, and the most important of his life.

Shortly before leaving, Shan returned to his home village, to bid his parents and brothers farewell. He spent most of that time helping them with the farm chores. When it was time to go, Shan's parents, making one of their infrequent trips into town, took part of the day off to accompany the boys to the train station in Jiaxing. Then Shan's brothers rode with him all the way to Shanghai, to see him off to "Meiguo."

"I'll come back to marry you," Shan had told Yang—as if there was never any question about it. And there wasn't.

Yang trusted him completely. "I'll wait for you," she had told him. And she did.

TWO

Upward Bound

Lu Gang was born in 1963, the only son of a rather ordinary couple in Beijing—his mother worked in a hospital clinic, and his father was a clerk in an automobile supplies shop. Lu had two older sisters, who doted on him. The family shared a tiny apartment in the residential compound of a military hospital known only as number 262.

Starting early in life, Lu had a rebellious streak that got him in trouble repeatedly. In kindergarten, he called Lenin a "bold ass." In junior high school he didn't hesitate to make his annoyance known when assigned to visit Chairman Mao's memorial in Tiananmen Square. It was around the time of final exams, and Lu didn't want to be bothered. For that, he was forced to deliver a self-criticism speech before the entire class. He was also stripped of his duties as vice leader of the class, and its representative for physics.

Lu was no sissy, but he was not especially athletic. While other boys played, he watched from the sidelines. When he was a child on a shopping trip with his parents, the family once happened upon a street fight among some hoodlums. When his parents stopped to watch, Lu tugged at his mother's sleeve, anxious to leave the scene: He preferred to go home and read. When his parents had friends over for dinner, he would excuse himself after the meal and go outside to the vegetable shed—with a candle and a book.

Although Lu was always a better-than-average student, he didn't excel until middle school, where he developed a keen interest in math and science. Then his grades soared to tops in his class. In high school, he captured numerous scholastic awards, then easily won admission to Beijing University. There, Lu was an academic standout during all four years, and as a result became eligible in autumn of 1984 (his senior year) to take a battery of examinations in hopes of qualifying to go to the United States to earn a Ph.D. in physics.

The bilateral program was a direct result of the Sino–U.S. détente started by President Nixon in the early 1970s. Shortly after Washington and Beijing established diplomatic relations in 1979, a Chinese-American physics professor at Columbia University, Nobel laureate T. D. Lee, working with Chinese education officials, created a special program to bring outstanding Chinese physics students to the United States in order to earn advanced degrees. At that time, however, China did not have The Graduate Record Examination (GRE) in physics, so there was no way to evaluate Chinese physics students.

Lee devised a test that became known in both countries by its acronym, CUSPEA—which stands for China–U.S. Physics Examination and Application Program. Comparable in difficulty to the GRE, the annual CUSPEA examination (which took three days to complete) was divided into three distinct parts: classical, modern, and general physics. The tests were graded by a special committee of about sixty physics professors from the Chinese Academy of Sciences.

Like Shan Linhua a year later, Lu scored in the ninety-fifth percentile, easily qualifying for one of the 120 slots. Soon he would become one of about 340 Chinese government-sponsored students studying in the United States under the auspices of CUSPEA and scattered among some 84 American universities—including the University of Iowa.

Because CUSPEA was a private, collegiate arrangement, the Chinese students had to compete on an equal footing with American, European, and all other entering graduate students. Initially, educators on both sides of the Pacific were highly concerned that CUSPEA students would not do well in America, given their lack of hands-on experience (especially in experimental physics). But the experimental physics majors proved just as capable and knowledgeable as the theoretical physics students. Both groups, in fact, scored in the upper percentiles in Ph.D. qualifying examinations at universities all over America.

For many of the Chinese students, including Lu, one of the most difficult barriers was the English proficiency test. Before being selected, each student had to pass a written English test, followed by two sets of interviews— one (on physics) with a Chinese panel, and a second (general) with a panel of American professors and their spouses, both of whom assessed the candidates' ability to communicate in English. Lu did significantly worse on the latter. But, given his outstanding physics score, the language panel let him slide past. After all, almost every successful CUSPEA student had to undergo intensive English training prior to departure.

And so, by the spring of 1985, Lu had every reason to be happy, and upbeat about his future. One of China's top physics students, he was headed for the United States, where he would most assuredly earn a Ph.D. And that particular ticket would guarantee him a prestigious lifetime job back in China—probably at Beijing University, the country's best. Instead, Lu felt perturbed. He already was coming to the conclusion that he had chosen the wrong career. While a star student at Beijing University, earning top grades majoring in space physics and astronomy, he had been determined to become a research scientist. But now, just as he was on the verge of this great triumph, the rules of the game were changing right before his eyes. Seemingly overnight, the masses had begun to worship Western-style capitalism—and astute businessmen were fast becoming more admired than educators schooled in either the classics or the sciences.

The prospect of conducting space research in what he had come to see as some drab laboratory with antiquated equipment at Beijing University was quickly losing its allure for Lu. That setup was not going to bring him the wealth and the comforts that he now coveted—and that so many of his less-educated countrymen already had attained. In short, Lu felt betrayed by the system, and his envy of those who were becoming fabulously wealthy began to grate.

Many of the newly rich didn't even have college degrees, and some could barely read or write. Yet they were making money at a breathtaking pace—twice, three times, ten times their normal salaries. This was truly unheard of! Was this what capitalism was all about? No wonder people all over the world emulated the American way, and ceaselessly searched for schemes to get into the United States!

In fact, within barely a generation things had practically turned upside down. When Mao Tse-tung assumed power in 1949, he effectively eradicated private enterprises, branding even the lowly street vendors as corrupt "tails of capitalism." But under his successor, Deng Xiaoping, rapid egalitarianism and rigid class politics were abandoned— and free markets began springing up like mushrooms after a good rain.

In Beijing, Lu was awestruck as he strolled through the noisy, colorful outdoor markets on Dongsixi Street, bustling with shoppers and small-time merchants even in the early morning hours. From behind a huge pile of cabbages, a vegetable farmer used an abacus to do his calculations—but the fisherman at the next table had a battery-operated digital scale for weighing sea bass. Everything from Coca-Cola to French cigarettes was available. So were the services of barbers, bicycle repairers, and handymen, most of whom roamed the neighborhoods in the evenings.

Thanks to Deng's economic policies, private entrepreneurs were racking up sales more than 100 percent greater than those of state-owned commercial enterprises. In the countryside, as peasants jumped on the bandwagon, television satellite dishes became a common (if seemingly out-of-place) feature that dotted the rural landscape. Inside many homes, which had pretty lace curtains and expensive parquet floors, the owners not only had large color TV sets but the latest VCRs as well. At the end of the day, the working family could sit back and, with their remote controls, select from a large menu that included Donald Duck yelling at his nephews—in Mandarin, of course.

All over China, a new class of well-to-do merchants was emerging. And soon they began hiring maids, cooks, and nannies (a practice once denounced as bourgeois extravagance but now blessed by official approbation). The newspapers were filled with propagandistic feature stories extolling those who had created yet another ingenious way of making it big under the new economic order. "Have No Fear of Becoming Prosperous," screamed one headline typical of the time.

The citizenry responded wholeheartedly. In 1982, while Lu was still an undergraduate, more than 2.5 million private enterprises obtained business licenses. But that number more than doubled in just one year. And by the time Lu was a senior at Beijing University, there were almost 10 million private enterprises in China.

In the newly fashion-conscious cities, tailors were in great demand again. Doctors and dentists set up private clinics. Teachers began moonlighting. Even prisoners could earn bonuses and extra pay for meeting production goals, as well as for good behavior, according to China-watcher Orville Schell's book *To Get Rich Is Glorious: China in the '80s*.

Even in relatively drab Beijing, Lu could see that China's mad rush to make money had begun to dramatically alter the city's skyline. Dozens of Western-style, high-rise hotels went up, complete with restaurants in gleaming atriums, around-the-clock room service, swimming pools, tennis courts, and health clubs replete with saunas, jacuzzis, and jogging tracks.

Designers like Halston and Cardin made high-profile tours of China, visits that quickly spawned a rash of Chinese fashion magazines. Beauty salons, once banished to the remote corners of Western-style hotels, proliferated. Plastic surgeons began doing brisk business, performing their magic on eyelids, noses, and even breasts. Furs costing more than $3,000 could be had without being tagged in any way shameful.

By 1985, the year that Lu left for Iowa, a dance craze became the latest fad, fueled by yet another American icon: the boom box. Lu didn't know how to dance, but he watched with bemused tolerance as other young people sweated away the hours doing such intricate footwork as the waltz, the rhumba, and the jitterbug.

The mass craving for all things Western—and especially American—was such that a U.S. novelty company selling deeds to 50 square inches of land in America (one inch in each state) did phenomenal business in China. The American Acres Inc. purchased an acre of land in each of the fifty states, divided its holdings into 6,272,640 square inches, and then marketed the deeds for $49.95 each as an offbeat novelty gift. In China, prices went berserk, fetching as much as $1,700 on the black market.

China was on the way to becoming the world's fastest-growing economy, and there was lots of money to be made. Yet Lu felt utterly excluded. His all-consuming studies at Beijing University had left him little time or energy to explore the modern-day gold rush. Instead, he was a mere bystander, marveling with undisguised envy at the astonishing pace at which fortunes were being amassed all around him. (Even the university's history department had opened its own gift shop!) But China's scientists were being left behind—a fact that weighed heavily on Lu. All he could envision were more years of hardship and sacrifice, for himself as well as the others. But for what? There was no question that the working conditions for China's scientific brain trust were abominable, and getting worse.

For those who had gone abroad earlier and were now back, things were somewhat better. They had faced relatively little competition upon their return, and therefore settled into decent—even cushy—work assignments. There had been, after all, a shortage of jobs in science and technology. "The overwhelming majority of Chinese research institutes are paying great attention to the persons who have studied overseas...by creating the conditions necessary for enhancing their newly developed skills," one Chinese newspaper boasted in the early 1980s. The early returnees were promoted quickly and played leading roles in teaching, and in research and development.

Eventually, with more scholars returning each year, competition for the best jobs intensified sharply, especially in desirable cities like Shanghai and Beijing. Instead of a manpower shortage, a scarcity of openings quickly developed, particularly at the best institutes and universities. As a result, many freshly minted Ph.D.s were assigned to work units without regard for their individual talents, expertise, experience, or desire. One survey found that as many as 20 percent of the returnees were stuck in jobs that did not even require the knowledge and specialization that the applicants had acquired.

Even a number of those who *did* find proper job placements were less than happy. Having trained at some of the world's top laboratories and research institutions, and thus accustomed to state-of-the-art equipment, they were shocked by the woefully inadequate facilities back home. "Scientists working inside China have long faced the double burdens of primitive working conditions (for example, old equipment and insufficient subscriptions to scientific journals) and a restrictive political environment," wrote Xin Hao, a visiting scientist from the National Center for Superconductivity Research in Beijing, in a 1992 letter to the editors of *Physics Today*, an American monthly scientific journal.

All in all, the plight of the Chinese scientist was abysmal—a fact widely known throughout the country, thanks to a rejuvenated press that was beginning to develop modest investigative tendencies. With each report, Lu Gang became further disheartened.

By far the most egregious complaint among scientists at this time had to do with wages. According to one survey of China's top thirty-six science institutes and universities, 80 percent of foreign-educated scholars were making less than 100 yuans a month; 10 percent with doctoral degrees were earning less than 78 yuans a month. By comparison, a midcareer urban high school teacher was earning an average salary of 100 yuans per month. (At the time, one Chinese yuan was roughly equal to 60 cents.)

The frustrations among the scientific elite were aggravated by the rigid seniority system. The spunky *World Economic Herald*, which enjoyed tweaking the establishment, went so far as to report in 1986 that only intellectuals in Kampuchea (formerly Cambodia) had to live with lower pay and worse working conditions than those in China. An exaggeration, perhaps, but the point was well taken.

By the early 1980s, only 50 out of 915 of China's best physics students who had gone to the United States to study came home as expected. And as he was preparing to travel to Iowa, Lu began contemplating what was once unthinkable: Maybe he too would become an expatriate.

Angry over what he now regarded as a wrong career decision, Lu blamed not himself but his parents. He privately faulted them for not having steered him into a more practical field, like medicine or business. Yet he understood that they were too ignorant on matters of higher education to have provided him with much guidance in that area.

Physics had been Lu's true love, but the prospect of making a fast buck was beginning to win out over his love of science. And so even as he accepted the University of Iowa's offer of a graduate research assistantship in physics, a plan began taking shape in his mind: After arriving in Iowa, he would abandon physics and take up business administration instead. *That* would be his ticket to a new and better life.

With fresh determination, Lu Gang sat down on a bitterly cold afternoon in the Beijing University library and began filling out his application for a student visa to America.

THREE

A New Beginning

More than twenty-four hours had passed since Lu Gang left Beijing, jostling his way aboard a jam-packed China Airlines jet bound for San Francisco. And now, jet-lagged after a connecting flight to Chicago and a brief American Eagle commuter flight to Cedar Rapids, Iowa, the twenty-one-year-old physics scholar was anything but excited about starting a new life in America. Rather, he was numb with fatigue.

On this hot and muggy summer eve, the immaculate passenger terminal at the Cedar Rapids Municipal Airport was almost deserted, except for the tiny clusters of families and friends on hand to greet the dozen-or-so arriving passengers. It was late, and the sole clerk in the gift shop was getting ready to close up for the night.

Behind the Avis Car Rental counter a bored, gum-chewing clerk reluctantly put down her dog-eared paperback book as a rumpled businessman, probably a farm-implements salesman, slowly walked up and let his battered suitbag crumple to the floor.

In a nook across the way, a well-stocked Iowa tourist-information booth was already abandoned for the night—

though anyone could still take advantage of its cornucopia of neatly arranged brochures and pamphlets that boasted of charms—both local and statewide—in breathless language that only a Chamber of Commerce publicist could dream up. But there were no takers on this August evening.

At the entrance to the men's washroom, a janitor nonchalantly stepped aside with his mop and bucket-on-wheels as a burly young man made a beeline for the freshly scrubbed facilities.

At the far end of the heavily air-conditioned terminal, near the exit, two uniformed airport workers appeared out of nowhere as the baggage carousel noisily cranked up.

This rather mundane scene struck no one but Lu Gang. Coming from a teeming nation of more than one billion people, he was accustomed to being surrounded constantly by a sea of humanity, especially in public transit facilities. America was going to take some getting used to.

The passenger terminal quickly thinned out as Lu stood waiting for his two large brown suitcases to appear on the carousel. Gradually it dawned on him that no one was there to pick him up. He was on his own. And this inauspicious beginning irked him, because the University of Iowa was still a good twenty-five miles away.

That spring, the university's Office of International Education and Services had been quick to get in touch with Lu after he was admitted as a doctoral candidate, airmailing him bundles of orientation material intended to smooth his transition to both the university and Iowa City. And one thing that the Office of International Education and Services had made abundantly clear to him—as to all other new foreign students—was that, with only five staff advisers to serve nearly 2,000 foreign students, it lacked the personnel to directly help each of them get settled. Especially at the start of the academic year, when everyone arrived in a crush.

To assist students from abroad in nonacademic areas such as orientation, financial planning, social adjustment, and intercultural activities, the Office of International Education and Services had only three general advisers, one immigration counselor, and an international activities coordinator. That was it.

Budget constraints aside, the university wanted foreign students to have as much direct contact as possible with American students. To encourage such town-gown, cross-cultural socialization, the office actively promoted a Friends of International Students program whereby a "host family" would take a foreign student under its wing, particularly during holidays—when the typical student from abroad had no place to go.

It was because of this combination of insufficient staffing and a desire to encourage self-reliance on the part of new arrivals from overseas that the assistance office advised foreign students to make their own travel arrangements, right down to securing a ride from the Cedar Rapids Municipal Airport to the university, and finding their own lodging. "The Office of International Education and Services staff cannot pick up students at the airport, but in some cases arrangements can be made for volunteers from a student nationality organization to do so," one of its advisories stated.

Like most foreign students, Lu made a good-faith attempt to follow such recommendations. But because of his poor command of English, he bungled the effort—in two ways. First, before leaving Beijing he sent a letter to the University of Iowa's Chinese Students' Association, simply announcing the date and time of his impending arrival in Iowa City, assuming that the group would find him a place to sleep until he could secure permanent shelter. As it turned out, he had misread the information sent to him by the university, and, instead of addressing his arrival letter to the Friendship Association of Chinese Students and

Scholars (the informal self-help organization made up of students from mainland China), sent it to a rival organization made up of students from Taiwan. There, the letter ended up in the waste basket. In any case, Lu had addressed the envelope *only* in Chinese, and by the time it got sorted out by the U.S. postal bureaucracy, it arrived too late to help him.

And now, standing alone in the eery stillness of the Cedar Rapids Municipal Airport terminal, a suitcase on either side of him, the slightly built young man from Beijing pondered his next step.

A shuttle van driver spotted him first.

"You goin' to the university?" the driver asked with a smile.

Lu did not understand the man the first time.

"Are you going to the University of Iowa?" the driver asked again, more slowly.

Lu knew the fare would be an exorbitant amount— about $18. The Office of International and Education Services had warned him, but he had no choice. He asked to be taken to the Iowa House, a university-owned hotel that occupied a portion of the vast Student Union building. With proper credentials, a newly arrived foreign student could check into the campus facility at any hour. And a room could be had for less than $30 a night, though one might have to share it with other new arrivals.

Lu rode in silence, lost in his thoughts as the van sped south on Interstate-380, enveloped by the black Iowa night. It was a good twenty minutes before the lights of Coralville, on the outskirts of Iowa City, came into view.

Soon the van exited I-80 onto Dubuque Street, and deposited Lu at the riverfront Iowa House. A well-appointed hotel, more like a Ramada Inn than the spartan dormitory that anyone might have expected, to Lu it was downright posh. It even had wall-to-wall carpeting and well-lit hallways.

After checking in and briefly taking stock of his surroundings, Lu turned in for the night. He slept with his clothes on, a money belt tightly secured around his waist. By the standards he was used to, the cash Lu had to pay for the ride in from the airport and for the night's lodging amounted to a king's ransom, and already he knew why credit cards were so popular in America. (Here, one could get by almost entirely with plastic—for example, gas stations, of all places, take credit cards, he had read somewhere.) In China, even local-currency credit cards were still something of a novelty, with no more than a few hundred thousand of the wealthiest Chinese holding such "renminbi cards." Now in Iowa, however, and with a $7,700, half-time physics department teaching assistant-ship already lined up for the coming academic year, Lu resolved to get himself maybe even several credit cards, just as soon as he got settled.

Americans might at that time have found $7,700 barely enough to cover minimum living expenses, but that was only because of their extravagant tastes, Lu quickly decided. Such a sum was more than enough for a frugal-minded, serious young man. He not only intended to get by on that sum, but also planned to send a good chunk of it home to his family in Beijing. As he began dozing off, Lu also dreamt about buying an American automobile. A sporty model just might be the thing that would impress the American coeds. As Lu slept on foreign soil for the first time in his life, he knew he had arrived. In the morning, after a satisfying, if unfamiliar, breakfast of eggs and bacon at the student union cafeteria, where he sat by a window overlooking the mud-brown Iowa River, Lu set out for his first real look at Iowa, his home for the next few years.

*   *   *

Iowa is perhaps best known as America's breadbasket, the country's number one corn producer, responsible for about a quarter of the national total. (Iowa is also the country's top producer of hogs and eggs.) Remote from either coast, the state has what meteorologists call "humid, continental" summers, which make for ideal corn-growing conditions. All over the state, colorful postcards showing nothing but fields of tall corn are available for purchase.

A less well known fact about Iowa is that more than 100 years ago its farm population had stopped growing. And by 1956, for the first time, more Iowans lived in cities than in rural areas. The urban growth was fueled largely by mechanization related to agriculture, which provided many new jobs in meat packing, poultry dressing, the production and processing of dairy and other farm products, and (most of all) farm tractors and combines. Throughout Iowa, small towns withered as the sprawling urban factories lured not only local residents, but also many farmers who realized that they could make more money off the farm than on. Often in far less time.

More than any other community in the state, Iowa City is regarded—derisively by some Iowans—as a liberal mecca rich with cultural and intellectual stimulation, but sometimes a bit strange. At Halloween time, for example, the school board encourages students not to dress up as witches, devils, slaves, handicapped persons, Indians, or even hobos—leaving not a lot of standard figures to choose from.

Iowa City was founded in 1839 as the territorial capital. But when officials decided to move the capital to the more centrally located Des Moines, they gave Iowa City the university as a consolation prize. Today, with its 30,000 students and 12,000 faculty members and other employees, the university dominates the easygoing, neatly organized, quintessentially Midwestern college town of some 65,000 residents. When the beloved Hawkeyes play a Saturday afternoon football game at home, even the Old Capitol Building (now a museum and a historical national landmark) shuts down.

In its modest, formative years, the university was often referred to mockingly as Johnson County High School, after the quality of its students—many of whom had barely mastered the three R's. Seeking to elevate academic standards, the school's first president, Rev. Jared M. Stone, created the Department of Natural Philosophy, which began offering courses on electricity, magnetism, meteorology, and the structure and dynamics of matter and energy. The department became the forerunner of what one day would become the world-famous Department of Physics and Astronomy, whose faculty members played a vital, military-oriented role during World War II. Still later, the department and its chairman, James Van Allen (a native Iowan), virtually became synonymous with space exploration—and it was that reputation which lured some of the world's finest physics students and practitioners to the University of Iowa.

* * *

As he set out into the muggy morning, Lu Gang's first destination was the Parklawn Apartments, a four-story red brick building on the other side of the river but just a short walk from the main campus. Over the years, the plain-looking conglomeration of housing units had become something of a ghetto for foreign students—especially those from China. Before leaving China, Lu had heard about the Parklawn from several scholars who had studied at the University of Iowa.

Behind the apartment building was a large parking lot, wherein Lu was impressed to see so many automobiles and bicycles parked. In one corner of the lot, several Chinese students were doing Tai-chi. In another corner was a neatly plotted community vegetable garden, complete with a makeshift irrigation system serviced by a garden hose that disappeared inside a ground-floor window.

It would be a nice place to live, Lu thought. But he was

too late; there were no vacancies for the fall semester. Luckily, however, the manager knew of a room that was available just a few blocks away. The one drawback was that it was more like a boarding house than a traditional apartment building, having just one bathroom on each floor, and a community kitchen for all.

Lu's shirt was drenched with perspiration by the time he reached 322 Ellis Avenue. From the outside, the three-story brick structure seemed attractive enough. But its white trim and little flower beds out front belied the seediness within. It might easily have been mistaken for a fraternity house, for the neighborhood was home to many of the university's fraternities—a fact that pleased Lu. It would be fun to be this close to the party-minded Greeks.

More than 3,000 students (14 percent of the student body) belonged to fraternities or sororities. Most of the 47 Greek chapters at the university emphasized service-oriented, civic, and community activities to a greater extent than did their counterparts at other Big Ten schools. But it was hard for them to shake the stereotypical image of fraternities and sororities as having little interest in much beyond having a good time.

Inside, the boarding house was old and run-down. Even the dark, narrow hallways couldn't hide the frayed orange carpeting, with its countless bare spots. Apartment No. 8 was predictably shabby. The tiny room, with its cheap wood paneling and dirty gray linoleum floor, measured no more than 10-by-15 feet. A minuscule recess in the wall served as the closet. This was no Iowa House, but at least the rent was reasonable—less than $150 a month, utilities included.

Lu was happy to take the room. Like graduate students everywhere, those at the University of Iowa cared little about their living conditions. After all, they spent so much of their days (and nights) in the library or lab. "Home" was just a place to sleep, and maybe grab a quick meal. Most foreign students at Iowa, like Lu, preferred off-campus accommodations to university housing. Still, there were drawbacks. Almost none of the individual living units were equipped with kitchens—a must for most foreign students, who often prepared their own native meals. But the biggest inconvenience of all, from the foreign students' perspective, was that all but two of the dormitories shut down between semesters. And that always was a time of unusual productivity for graduate students, a time when the last thing they needed was the distraction of having to find, and pay for, temporary lodging.

University officials lamented the clustering of foreign students in off-campus ghettos. Such isolation vastly reduced the time available for sustained interaction between American and foreign students. Unstructured opportunities for mutual exchanges were particularly beneficial to the foreign students like Lu, who desperately needed to practice their English. Despite his poor command of English, however, Lu would soon be starting work as a teaching assistant in the Department of Physics and Astronomy.

The inability of foreign teaching assistants to speak easily understandable English was a growing problem at the University of Iowa—just as at universities across the country. This was especially true in math and the sciences, fields inundated with foreign students. University officials, hardly unaware of the problem, attempted to ensure that minimum proficiency standards were met. But often this amounted to little more than lip service.

Inevitably, undergraduates became increasingly distressed, with some even taking their cases to the press. Typical was this complaint by Jonathan Schiller, a sophomore, who told the school newspaper, the *Daily Iowan*, that a teaching assistant in his statistical analysis class spoke such poor English that the instructor often had to communicate with the class by writing on the chalkboard.

Schiller and some of his classmates complained to the department, but to no avail. "It was almost worthless to go to class," said another sophomore, Gregor Ernst, complaining about a teaching assistant in his philosophy and human-nature class. And first-year student Sara Bovvy said of the teaching assistant in her quantitative methods class: "I cannot understand a word that he says."

Such public grumbling soon began to command attention in Des Moines, the state capital, and there was growing talk among legislators of imposing tougher English proficiency requirements upon foreign graduate students. Such students were required to take the Test of English as a Foreign Language (TOEFL), but university officials often looked the other way, even if a foreign student scored poorly on the examination. And that was the case with Lu.

Some University of Iowa officials later were surprised that Lu was awarded a half-time teaching assistantship, given his dismal TOEFL score. "It was really bad," said one top university official, expressing belated chagrin that Lu had been given the paying job.

Since its inception in 1963, TOEFL is now administered as many as twelve times a year in virtually every country in the world. It is taken each year by as many as 800,000 students who aspire to study in the United States. The test consists of a multiple-choice format focusing on listening comprehension, written expression, and vocabulary and reading comprehension.

Because he scored significantly below the 600 standard, University of Iowa officials required Lu to take additional training and tutorial in both written and oral English as soon as possible. If his proficiency did not improve, his teaching assistantship might not be renewed.

Lu was painfully self-conscious about his language deficiencies, but he knew whom to blame. The Chinese students who had a better command of English were from the privileged class. They had parents who were intellectuals and also had studied abroad. Plus, some even had enough money to hire tutors for their children. Lu felt like a poor little church mouse, the son of ignorant parents. Life, he decided, was really unfair.

*   *   *

Reverend Tom Miller's disciples repeated after him:

"A-E-I-O-U."

"Say it again—slowly," said Miller.

"A-E-I-O-U."

It was Saturday morning, and Reverend Miller was doing the Lord's work.

An ordained Baptist minister, Miller was a familiar figure on the University of Iowa campus, roaming widely in search of souls to save—those belonging to (among others) athletes, marching-band members, and international students. The conversion of Chinese students was to him something of a crusade.

The son of two Baptist ministers, Miller, now thirty-nine, grew up in Cedar Falls, where his father served as a campus minister at the University of Northern Iowa. After Miller married a clergywoman, they both did internships under his parents. Once he had completed his studies at the Bible College in Des Moines and the seminary in Grand Rapids, Michigan, the Millers moved back to Cedar Falls. But, seeking to branch out on his own, he began making weekly visits to Iowa City. In 1982, he and his wife and three children moved to the college town, and he joined the Faith Baptist Church located there.

In Iowa City, Miller's Campus Bible Fellowship group hosted a potluck dinner each autumn for the university's international students. To busy and cash-strapped graduate students, a free dinner was not something to be passed up lightly. And, much as most of the Chinese students found Western cuisine hard to stomach, they turned out in droves.

Soon Miller came up with another way to ingratiate himself with the Chinese students. Many, like Lu, lived off campus but had no automobiles. That left them pretty much at the mercy of the small convenience stores on the fringes of the campus, which charged higher prices than the suburban supermarkets. To help out the students, Miller—sometimes accompanied by his father—began taking them in his van on shopping excursions to the grocery stores, which are beyond walking distance from the center of town. Every Saturday morning, promptly at 10 o'clock, Miller would pull up at the Parklawn Apartments, or some other building where many Chinese students lived.

The occupancy turnover rate was high among the Chinese students, because they tended to move to better housing as soon as they could afford to—and were replaced by a fresh crop of their student countrymen. To Miller, this musical-chairs–like ritual greatly increased his exposure to potential new recruits. "We were practically the first Americans they'd meet," Miller recalled.

The motley crew of grateful students would pile into Miller's van for the ten-minute ride to the Econofood Supermarket on Broadway, just south of town. The group was usually back by 11 A.M. or so. Then, after the supplies were put away, Miller would convene a Bible study session. These rather informal gatherings, usually held in one of the student's homes, were not mandatory. But most of the students, having accepted a free trip to the grocery store, felt a certain obligation to attend.

"But it was no big deal," Miller said. "I'd begin while many of the students were still putting away their groceries. Some would come back; some didn't. People would just come and go."

The sessions were so low-keyed that occasionally Miller would play English teacher, "working with them on the vowels: A-E-I-O-U," the minister said. Other times, he would expound on some aspect or other of The American

Way. In time, Miller recalled, "many of us sincerely became friends, and I looked forward to Saturday morning." For the most part, though, Miller kept those early-weekend discussions centered around the Bible. He was realistic enough to recognize that many of the students were simply going through the motions, more interested in the steady rides to Econofoods than in God.

The one student who stood out was Lu. "He challenged almost everything my father and I said," Miller said. And they were surprised by Lu's gruff demeanor. "But that never fazed us," Miller added. "We didn't mind being challenged. That keeps our lectures interesting."

Lu challenged Miller to prove God's existence, and questioned the veracity of events described in the Bible. "How do you know that they are not just fairy tales?" Lu demanded to know at one point. "No Chinese student *ever* challenged us the way Lu Gang did," Miller said.

Lu's abrasive style also appalled the other Chinese students—and some privately apologized to the Millers for his behavior. But Miller truly was not bothered by Lu's questioning style. In fact, the two men developed something of a friendship, especially after discovering a shared passion for cars. Later, Lu even had Miller, his wife, and their three young daughters over for a home-cooked Chinese meal.

Another clergyman who got to know Lu was Jason Chen, a Chinese mainland-born immigrant who settled in Iowa City in 1967. As campus minister for the Christian Reformed Church, Chen had an office just across the street from Van Allen Hall, home of the Department of Physics and Astronomy. A friendly man in his forties, Chen frequently went to Van Allen Hall to use its copying center. Over time, he became acquainted with many of the physics students and faculty members, and began holding weekly brown-bag lunches with those interested in discussing religion.

Most who came to Chen's lunches were Chinese students. Lu was never among them—but he and Chen did end up having a memorable conversation over lunch elsewhere. On a chilly day in the spring of 1991, Chen and a Taiwanese student, a science major, decided to go for a buffet lunch at China Palace, a popular restaurant on the south side of town, near the Iowa City Municipal Airport. When the two men sat down with their plates, they noticed Lu at a table across the way, eating alone. So they invited him to join them.

Over the next forty-five minutes, the conversation turned to science and religion, and they began exploring the extent to which science and faith interacted. Was the Christian faith credible—particularly as it related to questions raised by science, such as Darwin's theory of evolution?

Lu threw out plenty of sharp questions. "He struck me as very bright and very articulate—a thoughtful, logical person," Chen recalled. "The intensity of that exchange was what I remembered. Lu Gang was very open. There was a mutual give-and-take. It was a healthy exchange. He was questioning, but not in the sense that he was trying to refute my Christian beliefs." Afterward, Chen decided that Lu was a student he would like to talk with again.

Lu's willingness to question and challenge authority was a trait that stood out in any crowd—especially among the Chinese students. But even in casual, everyday situations he often revealed a combative streak that he seemed unable to contain. He even argued regularly with roommates over which television network news broadcast to watch, sometimes spending the better part of the half-hour program to explain why he thought Dan Rather was better than Peter Jennings.

"He argued about everything, and he had this I-must-be-right attitude," said C.M., a one-time graduate student who for two semesters shared an apartment with Lu.

Returning home from class one evening, C.M. saw Lu out front, engaged in an animated discussion with a neighbor. The neighbor, also a Chinese student, didn't seem upset, but Lu was clearly in a state of agitation, highly annoyed at him. It turned out that they were talking about the concept of infinity, and Lu, as the science expert, felt that his neighbor, an engineering student, had the notion all wrong. Lu's eyes were glowering, and his face was flushed. He often got that way, even over the most inconsequential matters.

Although C.M., at nearly 6 feet and 180 pounds, was considerably heftier than Lu, who was 5-foot-4 and weighed 130 pounds, he learned to be wary of his volatile roommate, giving Lu a wide berth. In fact, unbeknownst to Lu, C.M. quietly began making plans to move out. C.M. also advised their other roommate to do the same. Nothing good will come out of their association with Lu Gang, C.M. told Shan Linhua.

Shan Linhua at the home of Erik Nilausen and Cheryl Tugwell in Iowa City. Christmas 1990. *Courtesy of Erik Nilausen and Cheryl Tugwell.*

Shan and Yilang Yang at the same Christmas party. *Courtesy of Erik Nilausen and Cheryl Tugwell.*

Shan and Yang with friends at a spring party.
Courtesy of Erik Nilausen and Cheryl Tugwell.

Shan declares his intention to become a Christian during the annual banquet of the University of Iowa Campus Bible Fellowship Club.
Courtesy of Tom Miller.

Rev. Tom Miller leads a Bible study group.
Courtesy of Tom Miller.

Shan at his commencement.
December 14, 1990.

Lu Gang was the physics
department's top student—
until Shan arrived.

Lu in front of the Tower Bridge, London, 1987.

Lu in London, 1987.

Lu in Paris, 1987.

Lu in Madrid, 1987.

Lu in Monte Carlo, 1987.

Lu in Vienna, 1987.

Lu, "the Cowboy," Las Vegas.

Lu, "the Cowboy," Denver.

Lu, during happier times, in a lounge at Van Allen Hall.

Lu, kibbitzing in Van Allen Hall.

Lu outside Van Allen Hall.

Lu protesting the killings of prodemocracy demonstrators in Beijing.

Lu demonstrating for free speech in Beijing.

FOUR

Looking for Love

With a thud, the bowling ball careened into the gutter, barely halfway down the alley. Lu Gang turned back with chagrin, grateful that there weren't too many other patrons nearby to witness his erratic game. As he waited for his ball to return, he took a seat at the scorer's table next to W.L., a fellow physics student from China. Undaunted by his mediocre game, Lu began expounding on his latest theories about the size and weight of bowling balls, and how best to use one's own weight to score well. But Lu's elaborate theories clearly didn't help his personal game much. As often as he bowled a strike or spare, he would roll the ball into the gutter. But W.L. humored his friend anyway, pretending to pay close attention.

The cliché one often hears about a student who excels is that he or she made it look so effortless. And that was certainly true of Lu. Faithfully, he put in the requisite amount of time toward his studies, his teaching responsibilities, and his own research. Yet Lu somehow also managed to end up with more free time than others. One of his favorite haunts was the Colonial Bowling Lanes out on Highway 21, a massive recreation complex with twenty-four Brunswick lanes, a roomful of pool tables, assorted pinball and video games, and even an indoor miniature golf course. Bowling was a new sport for Lu, but he had taken an immediate liking to it.

When he got tired of bowling, Lu would share a pitcher of Bud Lite with W.L., then drag his younger companion off to play miniature golf, another of his newfound passions. About the time that he had left for the United States, a full-size golf course was being built in China, amid much hype over the arrival of yet another Western pastime.

Lu was intrigued by the game of regulation golf, but had neither the time nor the money to take it up. However, on a certain autumn day he had gone out to Iowa's nearby Fairview Golf Course for a closer look. Although impressed by the serene beauty of the links, he was discouraged by the long line of people waiting for a tee time. With such a short playing season in his new home territory, the public courses were prohibitively crowded most of the time. And so Lu was delighted when he discovered the indoor miniature course at Colonial Bowling Lanes.

Lu never understood the chasm between indoor miniature golf and the real thing. But embracing the former was symptomatic of the many compromises he would make in his determination to adapt the American way.

*   *   *

It was Friday night and the Sports Column was rocking. The college hangout, just off campus, was especially popular among fraternity and sorority members, and tried hard to live up to its name. With two pool tables, a dart board, a practice basketball net, and a dozen large TV sets overhead (all tuned to ESPN), the Sports Column was a mecca for sports fans—but particularly for those who rooted for the professional teams in Chicago, the metropolis with which Iowa City identified. Interspersed with the hanging plants were the colorful banners of the Cubs, the White Sox, the Black Hawks, and the Bears.

The Sports Column, unlike so many college watering holes, actually had a bright—even pleasant—ambience, especially in the light of day. With high, beamed ceilings, the interior had a nice balance of wood and exposed brick, projecting a warm coziness that belied the raunchy nights when the bar became "a serious meat market," in the words of Jim Grutzmacher, a gregarious twenty-eight-year-old bartender and an off-and-on UI student. That was especially true, of course, on Friday and Saturday nights.

During the week, to generate business, the Sports Column sponsored hula hoop contests and limbo tournaments. They never failed to attract a bevy of pearly-toothed, peroxide blondes in tight-fitting jeans, who in turn attracted standing-room-only crowds of lusty—and beer-guzzling—young men. On Tuesday nights, a mug of cold beer from the tap cost just twenty-five cents. On Thursday nights, a sixteen-ounce beer went for only a dollar; it was called a "tall boy."

At the Sports Column, Lu drank pitchers of Bud Lite. Bowling and miniature golf might be fun pastimes, but the Sports Column was the place to meet the girls. Before even the first winter had set in, Lu had become a regular there, dropping in two or three times a week.

For many reasons, Lu stood out right away. He always arrived alone. And he was usually the only Asian in the barroom. Above all, he was noticed because of his quiet, almost meek, demeanor—a trait not found in great abundance at the Sports Column. "He was one of the real quiet customers," recalled Grutzmacher. "And because he was so quiet, he began to stand out. And a lot of us got curious about him."

Lu usually arrived at the bar—not even a full block from Van Allen Hall—around 9 or 10 P.M., just about when things began hopping. By then all the stools were taken and Lu, not being the pushy type, would hang back, standing behind the barflies. That's where Grutzmacher learned to spot Lu, who would always have a smile on his face and a couple of dollar bills in hand for a pitcher of brew.

"He didn't engage in much conversation, not even small talk," Grutzmacher recalled. "He usually just smiled." Because of his pleasant, if shy, demeanor, Grutzmacher and the other bartenders came up with an affectionate nickname for their inscrutable customer: Sweet Lu. Privately, Lu was quite pleased. It was a sign that he was beginning to fit in nicely.

Beer in hand, Lu would turn from the bar and patiently work his way toward the center archway that divided the Sports Column into two large rooms. There, by a pinball machine, he kept a silent, occasionally bemused vigil on the antics in both rooms, watching the girls as they moved about. Lu could make that pitcher of beer last two hours.

Usually, Lu stopped after one pitcher. But once in a great while he got himself a refill. Either way, he always left long before closing time. "He never got intoxicated or out of control," Grutzmacher recalled.

The legal drinking age in Iowa is 21, a restriction that gave rise to countless private parties at which age was no consideration. Word of such after-hours blasts circulated almost every night at the Sports Column. After a while, some of the guys began inviting Sweet Lu to their get-togethers. But he always begged off, mumbling with a smile some excuse about getting back to his physics research. That was what the regulars expected Lu to say, and he never surprised them. Lu was still struggling with his English, and that made it awkward both ways to engage in much of a conversation, especially in the noisy atmosphere of either a bar or a party. "He tried to fit, but he wasn't that outgoing and he didn't have fluent English," said Grutzmacher.

Making little social headway on the bar scene, Lu soon tried a new tack. He took out personal ads in the local newspapers, including the *Daily Iowan*, the university's five-days-a-week student paper. Lu advertised himself as an intellectual looking to share "good times and quiet moments" with an attractive female interested in movies and music.

A number of women responded, including two coeds who were roommates and described themselves as "two beautiful women." Roxanne, a pharmacy student, and Sheila, a nursing major, said they might be "interested in investigating further," but only if he could assure them that he had described himself accurately.

"What exactly are you looking for in those who respond to your ad?" they inquired. "We know precisely what we are looking for, and hope you will send your honest reply...." They also instructed Lu to send a recent picture. But (perhaps put off by the women's assertiveness) Lu didn't bother to answer. Another response came from D.A., a twenty-one-year-old local hairdresser with a high school degree. He did not find her desirable, either.

In time, however, Lu managed to ingratiate himself to T.N.—an attractive, redheaded undergraduate from Cedar Rapids who aspired to become a dentist. But T.N. was having trouble with physics. So Lu offered to tutor her— for free. And she gratefully accepted. He was too shy to suggest that they go to his apartment, and besides, Lu correctly sensed that T.N. probably wouldn't have accepted the offer. Instead, they met one afternoon a week at the Cottage, a popular bakery just around the corner from Van Allen Hall.

Over espresso and blueberry muffins, they talked physics—and eventually Lu invited her out for dinner. But she lied, telling him that she already had a date. T.N. actually felt awful when Lu seemed crushed by her rejection. But the truth of the matter was that she simply had no romantic interest in him.

That November, T.N. left a birthday card for Lu in Van Allen Hall. It had an upside-down bear and read: "You're a terrific friend...any way you look at it!" She added in her handwriting: "Thanks for all the help you've given me in physics—you're so intelligent!"

A month later, T.N. mailed Lu a Christmas card, again thanking him for his help. She had gotten a C in the course. It was what they both had hoped for: The grade paved the way for her admission into dental school. Lu never heard from T.N. again.

His inability to connect with women drove Lu to pornography. He began accumulating stacks of hard-core magazines. He even had a red-hot poster that he stashed under his bed. And strewn about in his apartment, from the bathroom medicine cabinet to his night-table drawer, were an odd assortment of fancy condoms, apparently purchased from public restroom dispensers.

During a semester break Lu took a bus to Las Vegas, where he delved further into the seamy world of the sex industry. When he returned to Iowa City, he talked boastfully about the casino scene in a way that embarrassed rather than impressed his friends—especially C.M., one of Lu's roommates.

As if he knew that his confidantes might not believe him about the trip, Lu also brought back a pocketful of snapshots—of himself in the company of show girls and, almost without doubt, prostitutes from the Strip. In one picture, a scantily clad, heavily made-up woman was sitting on his lap. He had a silly, self-conscious grin on his face. Pointing to these snapshots, Lu would call out their "prices": This one was $50. That one was $70. She was

$90. Finally, a disgusted C.M. told Lu to put away his pictures and shut up.

*   *   *

Despite his failure to gain social acceptance, Lu didn't cave in. He never quit going to the Sports Column, and as his English improved, so did his all-around self-confidence. Tentatively, he began trying to strike up a conversation with one or another coed. Now quite a familiar figure, especially in the usual watering hole, he was pleased to find that familiarity could breed acceptance, especially if one seemed receptive—and a few of the girls started to initiate chats with him. Sometimes they even invited Lu to their table, for a beer on *them*.

There were, among the friendlier female students, Kathy and Sharon and Jenny and Liz. But the most special of all was Lisa, a striking blonde nursing student with waist-length hair and an infectious laugh. One night, on impulse, she returned Lu's smile and engaged him in conversation. She felt sorry for the vulnerable, solitary young man with the thick glasses and oily hair. Then she invited him to join her and her girlfriends at the corner table against the far wall. Lu brought over his half-warm pitcher of Bud Lite and grandly offered it all around.

Lisa, who already had a steady beau, soon came to regret her well-intentioned, innocent gesture. "I befriended him because he always seemed to be alone and had no friends," she later recalled. "He began to hang around the table with me and my friends, and so I talked to him once in a while. We just kind of became acquaintances through the bar. But we never went anywhere together."

Before long, Lu was focused on her almost obsessively. First he began sending her friendship cards. Then, on her birthday, he sent a dozen roses and a bottle of champagne. Next came the telephone calls: Lisa would return home at the end of the day to find four or five messages from Lu on her answering machine. She never called him back; but even that not-very-subtle hint didn't deter Lu. After several days of not hearing from Lisa, and not seeing her at the Sports Column, he showed up at her apartment one night—unannounced.

Lisa was there all right. And so was her boyfriend. He told Lu in no uncertain terms to leave, and quit bothering Lisa. He also said that Lu was harboring a serious delusion if he thought she was attracted to him. In fact, he emphasized, she wanted nothing whatsoever to do with him. With that, the boyfriend slammed the door in Lu's face.

On his way out, an infuriated Lu kicked at the hallway wall. Thinking back to that incident, Lisa recalled: "He never threatened me, but he did scare me a few times."

The next time Lisa saw Lu, he appeared to be hanging around the parking lot of her apartment building. Fearing that he intended to vandalize her car, Lisa thought about calling the police. But soon Lu was gone. A few minutes later, she telephoned him at his apartment. He answered on the second ring, telling her that there was no one there by the name of Lu Gang. She hung up. A short time later, he called her and left this message: "We are through." Lisa sighed with relief. She never heard from him again.

"I felt bad for him. I always did," Lisa later said. "I thought he was kind of a nice guy and that he was just kind of lonely and was looking for a friend." But Lu Gang wasn't looking for just *any* friend. He was looking for an *American* friend. Why? No one could ever quite figure that out. "My *guess*," said the Reverend Mr. Miller, "is that in his own mind, an American girlfriend could somehow help him stay in the United States."

FIVE

Down to Business

Because of his social awkwardness, aggravated by a raging desire to assimilate, Lu Gang soon became known, at the Sports Column and even among the other Chinese students, as something of a misfit—albeit a benign one. But in his other life, as a physics scholar, Lu had a reputation of a different sort. Despite his language problems, Lu had easily established himself as one of the most brilliant graduate students at the Department of Physics and Astronomy. Ever.

"I'm willing to bet that Lu was in the top five," said Professor John Fix, who was Lu's first academic adviser. When Lu was assigned to him in the fall of 1985, Fix recalled a young man somewhat uncertain of which direction in physics research to undertake. "My job as an adviser is to make sure what a student's background is, get him started in the correct graduate courses, advise him on the proper sequence of courses, and maybe become his research adviser," Fix said.

With Lu, he had an easy time. Lu preferred to keep most things to himself. He never even disclosed to Fix—much less sought the professor's advice on—his desire to switch majors, from physics to business administration.

"He was very, very quiet. But that wasn't unusual. Many foreign graduate students—particularly the Chinese—are not very adept at the English language." Fix said. "So it wasn't all that unusual that Lu Gang did not open up. And, you know, the faculty here generally gets involved in the private lives of their students much less than people think. Basically, that's their own business. If they have a problem, fine. Otherwise, we try to avoid being intrusive."

Like many of the other senior faculty members, Fix occasionally had departmental social events at his home, and he always made sure that the foreign students, including Lu, were invited and made to feel genuinely welcome. "I never had an unpleasant encounter with him," Fix said in retrospect. Neither did Wayne Polyzou, a personable, forty-one-year-old professor who specialized in theoretical nuclear physics, focusing on the properties of protons and neutrons, and what holds quarks together.

In the fall of 1985, Lu enrolled in Polyzou's class on classical mechanics. A New Jersey native who earned a Ph.D. from the University of Maryland and did postdoctoral work at the Massachusetts Institute of Technology, Polyzou called Lu "one of the best students I've ever taught." Lu not only did exceedingly well on all the examinations, but also carried out every homework assignment with distinction. Once, Polyzou made a computation error on a problem that was a part of the homework. Lu not only caught his professor's mistake, but returned with the correct answer. "He came in and was very polite," Polyzou recalled.

Except for interaction in the classroom, that was about the extent of their conversations. "Lu knew that I thought he was a very bright student," Polyzou remarked. He ended up giving Lu an A+. "He was a full grade above an A, and I don't give them too often," said the professor.

Despite his singlemindedness when it came to theoretical physics, Lu was always ready to help others. Such problem-solving involved massive and complex mathematical calculations, and even a slightly erroneous assumption or seemingly minuscule miscalculation can set back a researcher for weeks—or more. Whenever a colleague was stumped, Lu was often the first to offer encouragement, come forth with a helpful suggestion, or propose some new, insightful way of looking at the problem. And this Lu did tactfully, in such a way that never made the other person feel inadequate or inferior. He seemed genuinely happy to help a colleague—eager to foster a spirit of friendly collaboration in what is too often a highly competitive, even cutthroat, academic atmosphere.

When immersed in his own research, however (and that was most of the time), Lu often went for hours without even looking up from his desk in the small, fifth-floor office in Van Allen Hall that he shared with other graduate students. He usually even begged off when the other students went out for a late afternoon beer at the Deadwood, a dark and seedy bar preferred by the more cerebral students who majored in English, philosophy, or physics. Lu preferred the Sports Column. In fact, his car's bumper prominently featured a sticker advertising the place.

It was a tribute to Lu that he continued to excel academically even though he was now far more enamored with making money than with creating research breakthroughs in physics. He was staggered by the casual wealth all around him, which most Americans seemed to take for granted. Even the poorest of students had better and more spacious housing than most people in China! And most already had accumulated the creature comforts and electronic consumer goods that people in China had to save half a lifetime for—fancy cars, big color TVs with remote controls and stereo speakers, VCRs, CD players.

At times Lu was beside himself with envy. And, feeling sorry for himself, he was more certain than ever that he didn't want to become a research physicist. He would go for an advanced degree in business administration instead. *That* was the ticket to success.

*   *   *

Margaret B. Brooke was the first university official to detect the dark, brooding side of Lu Gang that few knew existed.

As a program assistant and a foreign-student adviser at the university's Office of International Education and Services, Brooke was the person to see when a foreign student wished to change his or her student visa status. And, starting in the mid-1980s, more and more foreign students—especially those from China—were trudging up the steep embankment toward her office in the International Center, high on a hilltop on the west bank of the Iowa River.

For Chinese students studying abroad, the short-lived but caustic campaign against "spiritual pollution" back home that began in October of 1983 had come as another jarring reminder of the political vagaries of modern China. For Deng Xiaoping, it was an embarrassing admission that his open-door policy had allowed excessive Western influences to take hold. And now came the crackdown. In Beijing, female city workers were forbidden from wearing "unwholesome" ornaments or excessive makeup. Hair could not be worn below the shoulders. For men, mustaches, beards, and even sideburns were out. At the city's Central College of Arts and Crafts, according to Orville Schell, an author and longtime China observer, "long and strange" hairstyles were banned, and a barbershop was set up next to the registrar's office. But the upheaval lasted barely six months before the pendulum began swinging back.

Such cultural gyrations were a hallmark of Chinese history. Many of the students who came to the United States in the nineteenth century quickly took up Western ways—often with great exuberance, if not finesse. They hid their queues—braided locks like "tails"—and abandoned their traditional Chinese garb for Western-style suits. They even took up baseball and football. Before long, word of their behavior got back to China, and by 1881 the education missions were terminated, and all the students thereof yanked back to the homeland.

Until the mid-1980s, most of China's government-sponsored students and scholars willingly returned to the mainland after completing their studies. But with the growing internal political turmoil, coupled with the deterioration in job prospects for scientists, increasing numbers of Chinese students began searching for ways to delay their return. Most had come to the United States in the early 1980s, and now were completing their degree programs.

One way to avoid going home was simply to overstay one's visa. The well-informed student knew that (unless one committed a crime) he or she was unlikely to be tracked down for deportation by agents of the Immigration and Naturalization Service. Still, an illegal status could well hamper job prospects in the United States. Besides, it was becoming easy for them to legally prolong their stay simply by changing their student visa status. And so, increasingly, they sought that change in order to delay returning home. And in the autumn of 1986, Lu Gang was among those who paid an unannounced visit to Brooke.

Like most scholars from China, Lu Gang had a J-1 visa status, which comes with a "two-year rule" requiring holders to live outside the United States for at least two years after completing their studies before they can apply for reentry into the country as an immigrant. This rule was specifically designed to encourage foreign students to return home after completing their studies.

But, as Brooke learned in the fall of 1986, Lu had an unusual reason for wanting to change his visa status. He had barely settled into a chair in her office when he informed her that he was about to change majors. The

College of Business Administration, he announced, had accepted him as an M.B.A. candidate. But because the college was unable to award him a teaching assistantship, or offer any other form of financial aid, he desperately needed to find work. And, as a J-1 visa holder, he needed to obtain a special dispensation from the university before he could find a job. (In recent years, in part due to the widespread unemployment of domestic workers, foreign students have been subjected to increasing restrictions on outside employment, and for the most part were limited to working for their own institutions.)

Lu needed to earn at least $10,000 just to cover room, board, and out-of-state tuition. But Brooke explained to Lu that no full-time student could earn that kind of money, even by working twenty hours a week in food services. In any case, that was beside the point, she added. Under U.S. immigration laws, J-1 visa students were *not allowed* to change majors. It was that simple. "You're stuck," Brooke told him.

Lu was dumbstruck. Of course there *must* be a way, he insisted. There are *always* loopholes and ways to get around these bureaucratic procedures. "Sorry," she answered. "This is not China." As Brooke recalled, "He just sat there like a sack of flour. He didn't accept this easily." In fact, Lu proved extraordinarily persistent, questioning her from every angle: Had she thought of *this*? Had she thought of *that*?

"He was polite, but not a very cordial person," Brooke offered in faint praise of Lu's tactics. On his way out, she recalled, he would take a few steps, stop abruptly, spin around, and throw another question at her. "He viewed our rules and our laws as impediments," she said. By the time Lu finally left her office, Brooke sensed, he was an agitated young man, resentful and scornful of the American way.

"Lu just couldn't understand that, in fact, laws and regulations do close off—no matter how much you try to fine-tune your tactics," said Gary Althen, a twenty-year veteran at the university's Office of International Education and Services, where he was assistant director for foreign students and scholars.

* * *

Lu returned to see Maggie Brooke at least half a dozen times, determined to find some glitch in the system that would enable him to pursue an M.B.A. But there was none. He even tried to finesse a transfer to the university's Department of Electrical and Computer Engineering—but there, too, he was stymied. There was no way out. Lu was boxed in.

Adding to his sense of injustice, Lu's $7,700 half-time teaching assistantship wasn't renewed after the first year. While some speculated that his language deficiencies may have had something to do with it, federal financial aid was definitely being cut back all across the country. There were just too many deserving scientists, researchers, and graduate students—as well as Big Science projects—competing for a shrinking pool of money.

Lu then applied for, but was denied, a graduate tuition grant, and complained bitterly about this rejection to Barbara Clark, another foreign-student adviser. Lu turned a deaf ear to her explanations, and found little solace in the fact that—as Clark pointed out to him—he nevertheless *had* been awarded an $8,500 graduate research assistantship. And it was virtually impossible for a graduate student earning more than $3,000 to get a tuition grant.

Lu was nevertheless not mollified, and continued trying to carry his case up the ladder of command. But there were no more rungs to be reached and stepped on. And this caused his level of anger and frustration to rise to a point where soon what was left of reason within him would first dip and then drop perilously—as if in equal and opposite reaction.

SIX

Rising Star

Despite the growing frustrations in both his academic and his personal life, Lu Gang continued to excel during his second year of graduate studies. That fall, he came to terms with the reality that he couldn't obtain an M.B.A. Doing business and getting rich just weren't in the cards. There was no choice but to push on. If nothing else, a Ph.D. in physics would be a high honor for the entire Lu family. And so he vigorously channeled his energies into his work, determined as never before to outshine the other eighty or so doctoral candidates in the department.

No one was more impressed with Lu's drive and brilliance than Professor Christoph K. Goertz, a theoretical space physicist born in Danzig, Germany, who was his new academic adviser. Goertz's internationally acclaimed research dealt with Jupiter and Saturn, and he had authored numerous scientific articles on the aurora borealis—the Northern Lights—also.

A lanky, bespectacled man who liked to dress casually, Goertz often showed up for class in jeans and an old cardigan sweater. He let his silver-gray hair grow over his ears, and wore a thick mustache that curled down just below the corners of his mouth—from which a cigarette often dangled.

Seeking to unlock the mysteries of how thin, charged gases, flowing outward from the Sun, are heated in the Earth's magnetosphere was one of his passions. "It's like a puzzle. I would like to know the answers—hopefully before anyone else. There is a sense of competition that is very strong in this field, as well as a strong sense of awe," Goertz once explained. "If you have ever seen an aurora, it's a spectacular and beautiful phenomenon. I'd like to know what is going on there." Goertz also made time to edit the *Journal of Geophysical Research—Space Physics*, one of the leading publications in the field.

Having an appreciative mentor, and one who was so prominent in his field, was a great source of satisfaction for Lu. His year got better still as he not only made straight A's but also began to be consulted by faculty members about prospective graduate students from China. *That* really made him feel important. Too, Lu had found more desirable living quarters.

Although he still spent little time at home, Lu was glad to be out of the dismal apartment on Ellis Avenue. He was now living in a smaller, two-story clapboard house on Church Street, where there were fewer people with whom to share the much-desired living space. Being on the east side of the river, it also offered a shorter trip to Van Allen Hall.

But easily the best part of the year came that spring, when Goertz invited Lu to accompany him to an international conference on space physics. The meeting was scheduled for June, right after school let out. And it would be held in Paris!

"He was very lucky. Not everyone takes students along for a trip overseas," Ulrike Goertz, the professor's wife, said of Lu—who could hardly believe his good fortune. Maybe he had made the right decision after all, in sticking with physics! Lu quickly began plotting an extensive tour of Western Europe. After almost two years in Iowa, he had planned to go home that summer to visit his family in Beijing. But now he was off to see the world. His family would simply have to wait.

In Paris, Lu diligently attended all the scientific sessions. But he spent most of his free time sightseeing. He rode the Metro all over Paris, and walked the streets late into the night, stopping for café au lait here and there. It was the most stunningly beautiful city Lu had ever seen. Up and down the Champs Élysées he strolled, gaping not so much at the shops that lined one of the world's most fabulous boulevards as at the carefree, nubile French girls everywhere. From the Arc de Triomphe he walked to the Eiffel Tower, crossing over the Seine at the Palais Royal. The views were spectacular at every turn. Lu had never quite felt such a sense of discovery before.

When the Paris conference ended, Lu and Goertz parted company. Lu was taking much of the summer off for his grand tour, even though he knew that Goertz didn't approve of his spending most of the summer "playing" in Europe. But Lu was unable to contain his desire to see as much as he could, time and money allowing. And, at least to some extent, Goertz understood Lu's intense curiosity— and his determination to "see the world." How often, after all, could a lowly paid physics graduate student from China get to see so much in so short a time?

From Paris, Lu took a train to Versailles. He had never seen anything so magnificent. Next was Marseilles, where he saw some of the prettiest girls he had ever laid eyes on. While other tourists took snapshots of the sights, Lu surreptitiously took pictures of French girls as they stood on the street corners or sat in the sidewalk cafes.

From there, Lu visited Barcelona, Berlin, Geneva, Madrid, Monte Carlo, Monoco, and Vienna. He even took a train through the Alps. For the most part, he looked no different than any other tourist, and yet he did stand out. Not only did he travel alone, but he went everywhere lugging a tripod for his camera. Using the tripod and a remote trip switch, Lu took pictures of himself posing before world-famous landmarks all over Europe. In many of these photographs, he could be seen with a key chain, bulging with keys, dangling heavily from his belt.

Lu's tour ended in London, which he explored thoroughly on foot, repeatedly crossing and recrossing the Thames on the city's numerous bridges. He took pictures of himself in front of Buckingham Palace, on the Tower Bridge, at the entrance to the British Museum, and under Big Ben, hard by the Houses of Parliament. He even took a picture of himself at the Royal Greenwich Observatory.

By the time Lu returned to Iowa City in the late summer of 1987, he seemed like a new person. He was energized, and optimistic once more about the future. Under Goertz's wing, he made steady progress toward his Ph.D. as the department's top student. With two academic years now under his belt, he was also a department veteran, someone other students looked up to—especially the newly arrived from abroad, and particularly those from China. Lu, in short, now had status. Life once again had meaning.

But Lu's newfound happiness didn't last long. When the fall semester began, a new and imposing presence suddenly achieved orbit in his system. And Lu soon came to the shattering realization that he was about to be eclipsed.

SEVEN

Roommates

Shan Linhua enrolled at the University of Iowa as a Ph.D. candidate in the fall of 1987, having transferred from Texas A&M University. With more than 40,000 full-time students, Texas A&M was the third-largest university in the United States, after Ohio State and the University of Texas at Austin. Over the years, the once all-male, all-military university had developed a top-notch College of Science, with an active program in theoretical physics. But Shan became increasingly drawn to space physics in particular, and Iowa had one of the best such programs in the world. So he made the move after just one year. At Texas A&M, Shan had established himself as the top graduate student in physics—and he had every intention of maintaining that status at the University of Iowa.

When he arrived in Iowa City, Shan—a cheerful person by nature—had special reason to be happy. In December, he would be returning home to marry his sweetheart, Yang Yiling. During their year-long separation, Shan had written to her every week, composing half the letter in Chinese but the other half in English. It was his way of encouraging Yang to get on with her English studies even before arriving in the United States.

Right from the start, Lu instinctively kept a close eye on Shan. And it was easy enough—they already were studying under the same professors. They even had adjoining desks in an office reserved for graduate students on the fifth floor of Van Allen Hall. It was as if the department, however unintentionally, had put Lu and Shan side by side, like thoroughbreds competing in a race for the highest stakes.

One day, Lu approached Shan and invited him to become his roommate. Lu had just signed a year's lease on a one-bedroom apartment in a three-story building on South Dubuque Street. It was just a few short blocks from campus, and there was an East-West Oriental Foods grocery store nearby. Lu already had one roommate there—a certain C.M. Lu slept in the living room and C.M. occupied the bedroom, which had a queen-sized mattress on the floor. The rent was $270 a month and, if split three ways, the cost would be uncommonly inexpensive. Like all the other Chinese students, Shan was obsessed with saving money, but he felt an even greater urgency since he would be paying for his wedding. So he readily agreed to move in.

Lu presented the arrival of a third roommate to C.M. as a fait accompli. He simply brought Shan home one evening and introduced him to C.M. as a new transfer student who needed a place in which to live. An easygoing person, C.M. went along with the new arrangement. (Working on a master's degree in biomechanics, he also was trying to scrimp. He hoped to save enough money to bring his young bride, who was still in Beijing, to Iowa.)

That the entire apartment measured only 16-by-35 feet mattered little to the three young men. They were rarely there—often gone well before 8 A.M. and not returning until 10 P.M. or later. "We spent eighteen hours a day on campus—either in a classroom, a lab, or the office," C.M. explained. "We just needed a place to sleep." He usually saw his roommates for no more than perhaps a few hours a day.

The sleeping arrangements were dictated by Lu: Shan and C.M. would share the bedroom; he would remain camped out on a couch in the living room. One restless night on the shared mattress, however, was all C.M. could take. The next morning, the bleary-eyed student went to a Goodwill store downtown and bought himself a used, twin-sized mattress.

Otherwise, C.M. didn't mind sharing a room with Shan. "He was a good fellow," C.M. said. Cramped as their bedroom was, both men made a special effort to keep the room neat. By contrast, the living room was a hovel. Lu's dirty laundry was scattered everywhere, as were his books and stationery supplies. It was as if he had no sense of personal hygiene—much less any regard for his room-mates. The shared kitchen was worse: Lu left a heap of food-encrusted dishes piled ever higher on the food-stained counter.

Garbage overflowed from the trash basket, and Lu never took it out. "Grease was literally dropping off the ceilings," recalled Harry Hinkley, the apartment's owner. Inevitably, cockroaches invaded—sure to be followed, C.M. feared, by rats. But even after Hinkley stepped in, ordering the occupants to literally clean up their act, Lu still refused to help C.M. and Shan with the chores.

C.M. had met Lu in the summer of 1987, just before the fall semester began. He had been living in a boarding house on East Market Street, but it was seven blocks from the Engineering Building—too far a commute for C.M. in the long, bitterly cold Iowa winters. One day he noticed a flyer in Chinese that advertised for a roommate to share an apartment that was much closer to the campus.

In between classes, C.M. went over to look the place over. The carpet could have used a good washing but the apartment, overall, was in good enough condition. The location was great, just up the hill from the Engineering

Building. And C.M. was happy to have the bedroom to himself.

C.M. thought that he kept long days, often not getting home from the lab or the library until 10 P.M. or later. But Lu was even more of a night owl; he frequently didn't return home until as late as 2 A.M. C.M. soon realized, however, that Lu wasn't necessarily out studying until the wee hours. In fact, Lu often was red-faced and reeking of beer when he swaggered in. One night, C.M. was in fact jarred awake by Lu, who came home steaming mad, muttering something about a woman named Liz who had snubbed him at the Sports Column. Lu even kicked a hole in the dry wall of the living room.

Shan occasionally joined Lu in going out for a late-night beer or two, and they always invited C.M. to go along. But C.M. invariably begged off, citing his work as an excuse. In fact, he despised Lu, and wanted as little to do with him as possible. To C.M., Lu was a self-centered know-it-all who thought he was better, smarter, and more with-it than any of the other Chinese students.

"He never respected anybody—not Tom Miller, not our neighbors, not his professors, and not me, even though I'm older," C.M. recalled. "He looked down on people and made fun of them behind their back. He believed he was the smartest person in the physics department, and felt everyone else should worship him and kow-tow to him. And he wanted the other Chinese students to listen to him because he felt he had America all figured out. Lu Gang was not a nice person."

On the other hand, C.M. became genuinely fond of Shan. "He was a very impressive guy. He respected people. He had a sweet personality. And he was really smart," C.M. said.

Even though Shan was engaged and had no serious interest in other women, the coeds invariably were more drawn to him than to Lu, and this became an increasing source of irritation to the latter. Finally, late one night, Lu stormed into the apartment in a rage. It turned out that both he and Shan had good-naturedly vied for the attention of a pretty coed, but she had responded only to Shan. From then on, relations between Lu and Shan began to cool. "I think Lu became quite jealous of him," C.M. said.

C.M. was especially touched upon discovering that Shan was subsisting on little more than bread and milk. Appalled, he incessantly urged his roommate to eat more meat and vegetables—but to no avail. Shan persisted in his monk-like existence. Again he explained that he was saving money to finance his own marriage, and didn't want to impose a financial burden on either his own family, or Yang's.

By late December, C.M. had moved out. His wife had arrived in Iowa City, and they had found an apartment in a university family-housing project. Elated to be leaving 528 South Dubuque Street, C.M.'s parting advice to Shan was that he, too, should move out. Lu Gang will bring nothing but trouble, C.M. told him. Shan nodded; he couldn't disagree with that assessment. He told C.M. he'd think about it—and he did. Within weeks, he also moved out, leaving Lu alone and increasingly isolated.

☆   ☆   ☆

Almost from the day that he arrived in Iowa City, Shan proved to be immensely popular—well-liked throughout the physics department, but especially so within the closely knit community of students from China. Quite aside from his outstanding scholarship, which quickly won rave reviews led by Chris Goertz, the exuberant Shan also became such a catalyst for good times that within a year of his arrival in Iowa his fellow Chinese students elected him president of the Friendship Association of Chinese Students and Scholars.

Shan organized Friday night basketball games at the Field House. On Saturday and Sunday afternoons, when the weather was nice, he got people to come out to play soccer. During the long winter months, Shan hosted parties in his home, to watch football games on ESPN. He was one of the few Chinese students who subscribed to the around-the-clock sports cable channel. And he became known affectionately as "the consultant" because only he seemed to fully understand the finer points of American football. He delighted in explaining to his buddies the intricacies of the game, and such imponderables as the difference between a touchback and a safety, and between a point-after-touchdown and a field goal. Many came not so much to watch a football game as to share in the good times. Of course, there were also card games, and plenty of good food to go around. (The younger generation *did not*, however, play mah-jongg.)

Before Yang arrived in Iowa, the guys would send out for pizza, and Shan would always insist on paying. After Yang arrived, she happily cooked for the guys, often with Shan looking with great interest over her shoulder. Yang was bothered only if Shan had more than a beer or two over the course of an afternoon.

In time, many of Shan's friends actually developed a keen interest in both college and professional football, thanks largely to his enthusiasm. And one of them, Fan Fan, a biochemistry major from northern China, actually split the cost with Shan on a ticket for the Hawkeyes' basketball season. "Shan was a very easygoing, very warm-hearted person," Fan said. "He was very considerate of others."

When Fan returned to China for a six-week home visit, Shan asked him to deliver some ginseng to his parents, which Fan did happily. When Fan returned, Shan immediately had him over for dinner, to show his appreciation.

Fan's first contact with Shan was in the early summer

of 1988, shortly after Fan, then twenty-one, was accepted by the University of Iowa. He had written the Friendship Association of Chinese Students and Scholars, asking whether someone could pick him up at the airport in Cedar Rapids. Within days, Fan received a warm welcoming letter from the group's new president—Shan Linhua. "Congratulations!" Shan wrote from Iowa. "It's very nice here." Shan also included the association's office telephone number for Fan to call when he arrived in the United States.

Only after being at the university for a while did Fan appreciate just how expeditiously Shan had responded to his inquiry. "I later learned how much people here like to just use the telephone and not write very much. So it was very good of him to have answered me so promptly," Fan said.

As it turned out, however, when Fan landed at the Los Angeles International Airport and called the association's office, the telephone there had been disconnected. The group had relocated several days earlier, and had not yet been given a new phone number. Thus, upon arriving in Cedar Rapids, Fan met up with another Chinese student at the airport, and the two made their way to Iowa City together.

After they met in person a few days later, Shan was profusely apologetic about the telephone mixup—but Fan was hardly upset about it. "He's a very caring person, and that's been an inspiration to me to help other people," Fan said. The two became fast friends, even in spite of trying to best the other in competition on the basketball court.

Fan later became editor of the association's newsletter and, working with Shan, introduced various new features, including restaurant reviews and coverage of the arrival of new Asian grocery stores in town. "Shan was always giving me fresh ideas," Fan recalled. Shan also wanted to start a column on breakthroughs and advances in science.

Through Shan and his own role in the friendship

association, Fan quickly got to know most of the other Chinese students at the university, by sight if not by name. Thus he was surprised one autumn night when he and Shan were at a party and he noticed the unfamiliar face of a quiet young man who stood more or less in a corner, off by himself. Later in the evening, Fan introduced himself to the stranger, who was still nursing his first bottle of Bud Lite. It was Lu Gang.

Although Lu seemed a loner by nature, he nevertheless joined in *some* group activities from time to time. Thus he and Fan gradually became acquainted, usually running into one another over dinner at a mutual acquaintance's house. "He was kind of isolated, but if you just met him a couple of times, you wouldn't recognize anything strange about him," Fan recalled.

After he broke his glasses one day, Fan decided to drive to Moline, about 60 miles away, to get contact lenses at an outlet that was having a sale. Hearing about the low prices, Lu and another mutual friend piled into Fan's car on the spur of the moment for the ride. Unfamiliar with the route, Fan was happy to have the company.

A few weeks later, Lu invited Fan over for dinner, which he cooked himself. After a tasty meal, Lu popped a video into his VCR. It was *Pretty Woman*, the movie (starring Julia Roberts and Richard Gere) about a prostitute who ends up with a dashing, well-to-do patron. Even though it wasn't the first time that Lu had seen the movie, he howled appreciatively throughout, until tears came to his eyes.

In one of his early years at the school, another of Lu's rare dinner guests had been An Tao, a twenty-eight-year-old fellow physics graduate student. Lu didn't like playing basketball, so tried to avoid it, but An (who did like it) occasionally accompanied Lu either to play miniature golf or to bowl at the Colonial Bowling Lanes. Afterward, Lu would invite him over for a home-cooked meal.

Like Fan, An Tao had met Lu at a gathering of Chinese students. In An's case, it was a party in Shan's home at the Parklawn Apartments. At one such gathering, Lu sat in a corner with Yang, seeking her advice about women. Yang eventually came to think of Lu as a friend.

Like so many Chinese students during the long Midwestern winters, An spent lots of Saturdays and Sundays at Shan's place. It became a home away from home, something of a tribal refuge from the world at large. Some would even drop by in the late afternoons during the week and wait for Shan to come home while Yang, periodically glancing out the window toward Hancher Auditorium down by the river and hoping to spot Shan walking across the parking lot, prepared dinner.

Lu appeared to be as interested as anyone else in joining in group activities, but his aloof and somewhat haughty manner put people off. "He seemed to like contact with the others, but it was just the way he behaved. He considered himself a little better than everybody else," An recalled.

When spring finally came to eastern Iowa, the Chinese students were anxious to revel in the wonders of the fresh outdoors. One sunny Saturday, about a dozen of them spent the better part of the day canoeing and pinicking out on Lake MacBride, a man-made recreational spot surrounded by 2,100 acres of parkland about fifteen miles north of town. Everyone had a delightful time, thoroughly enjoying a much-needed respite from grueling academic demands. There was not one sour note. None, that is, until the time came to calculate each person's share for the cost of the food and the boating fees.

Divided evenly, the tab came to $22 a person. But Lu protested. That sum, he said with agitation, did not include the $4.50 he had paid for a bag of potato chips and two bottles of soft drinks. He insisted that his contribution also be divided equally among the group. Never mind that one of the soda bottles was already half empty when Lu showed up for the outing.

Lu also insisted that the cost of several roles of film, plus developing, be prorated on the basis of how often a person had been photographed that afternoon. Everyone laughed at Lu's logic, some thinking that he was joking. But he was dead serious—and getting angrier by the minute because the others, challenging his reasoning, refused to go along.

"That's when the breakdown began," An recalled. Lu's bizarre behavior after the canoe outing became the talk of the Chinese student community. "I had a lot of friends in the physics department," Fan added. "And they got along pretty well with Lu Gang. But after that, some of them began to ostracize him. They felt he was strange."

Lu further alienated himself during a trip to Chicago. By then, he had bought himself a sporty, blue-gray 1985 Chrysler Laser that was unremarkable except for the bumper sticker on the back that said: "I'd rather party at the Sports Column." Lu drove two other Chinese students to Chicago because one of them wanted to buy a car there. While they were in the Windy City, however, a dispute arose between Lu and the others over who would pay for dinner. The facts never quite got sorted out, but Lu ended up abandoning his passengers in Chicago and driving home alone—a distance of more than 200 miles.

A few days later, the three men ran into each other at a party and resumed their argument, shouting with angry voices that left everyone else uneasy. Afterward, a sullen Lu sat down beside Fan and silently watched him finish a game of chess. "You just really got the feeling that Lu was alone," Fan recalled. "It was easy to mix with people. Everyone was pretty friendly. You really got the sense of one big family. But if you wanted to isolate yourself, you could. And Lu did—more and more."

But Lu's isolation had less to do with his tendency to

be a loner than with his inability to get along with people, and this was exacerbated by his abrasive personality and a certain rigidity that seemed to blind him to the consideration of others. In fact, Lu very much enjoyed the company of others. "It was important to him to be invited back after he had someone over for dinner," An said. And when Lu himself was a dinner guest, he would unfailingly show up at the doorstep carrying beer or a well-prepared dish.

In the spring of 1988, Lu and several classmates attended a physics conference in Boston. Afterward, they decided to go do some sightseeing in Washington, D.C., before returning to school. And Lu was determined to take a tour of the White House; he wanted to compare it to the Versailles, which he had seen a year earlier. But when the group showed up at 1600 Pennsylvania Avenue, the line of tourists extended from the east entrance all the way down to the Ellipse. It would be hours before they even reached the gate.

"This isn't worth the wait!" Shan objected. "Let's go see some other sights instead." But Lu refused to budge, especially after sensing that the others were ready to follow Shan elsewhere. "You go if you want," Lu snapped petulantly, "but I'm staying right here."

Happily, Shan and the others left, walking off toward the Washington Monument and the Mall. It wasn't until more than two hours later that the meanderers returned to the White House. There, much to their amusement, Lu was *still* in line. He glowered as they laughed and rejoined him—just in time to be admitted for the tour.

By early winter of 1991, Lu had become such a social pariah that almost no one came to his Chinese New Year's party, leaving him crushed—and angry. Shan, by contrast, could not have been more popular. He was one of those people that others liked to be around. "Entertaining almost became his hobby," said Feng Wei, a fellow physics student.

But Shan did a lot more than just study and party. He

viewed himself as a citizen of the world. When China
suffered massive flooding one spring, he started a campus
donation drive, using as seed money $50 of his own. The
effort resulted in several hundred dollars in relief funds for
the victims.

Not long before Yang arrived in Iowa City, Shan signed
up with Friends of International Students, the host-family
program sponsored by the university's Office of International Education and Services. The cultural exchange
program sought to bring together foreign students with
local residents who would take a special interest in the
collegians. Many foreign students signed up to be introduced to one or another host-family, but there was always a
long waiting period because of a constant shortage of
volunteer families from the local community.

An Tao's fiancée needed such help. After she arrived
from China and signed up, her first "hostess" proved to be a
pleasant and well-meaning woman who held a demanding
job in the Iowa City government but had little time to
devote to her charge. They finally met after several
months, and that was over a somewhat rushed dinner. A
second "hostess" was a business executive who was even
busier. "Everyone means well, but Americans just don't
seem to have the time," said An Tao.

The university tried (and of course still does) to foster
the host-family program, as well as the "nationality organizations," but there was (and is) just no way for the
understaffed Office of International Education and Services to do everything possible to help the steadily growing
number of foreign students arriving each autumn.

When An landed at the Cedar Rapids Airport in 1989,
for instance, he had trouble using the pay phone to call
Iowa City, where he hoped to reach a fellow Chinese
scholar already at the university. Before leaving China, An
had acquired from returned students a jumble of supposedly practical information about the United States. But

much of it proved either inaccurate or out-of-date. No one
had told An that calling Iowa City from Cedar Rapids
would cost more than thirty-five cents.

An finally was rescued by two women from Iowa City
who were at the airport to drop off a relative headed for
California. They gave him a ride to the university, and even
helped him to locate the scholar, who put An up for the
night.

An's first night in town was a revelation. He was
grateful for the hospitality, but shocked by the living
conditions. In a small house with seven sleeping units,
there were as many as three Chinese students to a room.
The place had suffocatingly low ceilings and was overrun
by cockroaches.

However, as An quickly learned, by living in such
squalid conditions the students had to pay only a mere
fraction of the rent required by most any housing alterna-
tive, off or on campus. Thus many Chinese students—in
that house and elsewhere—had a fat savings account that
belied their station in Iowa City.

An Tao lasted one night in that boardinghouse. But his
arrival experience was hardly unusual. "Most of the time,
the Chinese students have to ask the older students. Most
of us don't know all the advantages, and our English is not
good enough to find out about all the conveniences here,"
An said. "It's only after a year or two that we have a chance
to learn for ourselves."

When Shan signed up for the Friends of International
Students program in 1988, he had much better luck than
did An Tao and his fiancée. Shan soon was paired with a
remarkable couple in a match that seemed made in heaven.

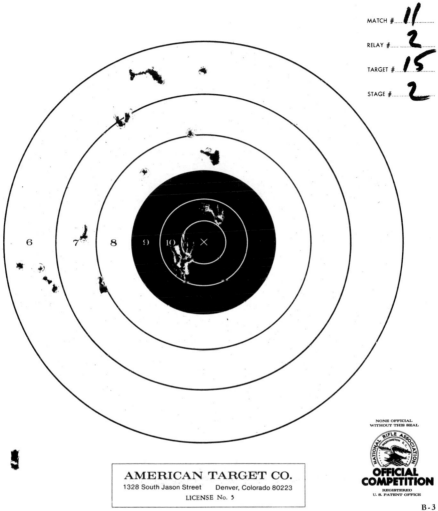

National Rifle Association

OFFICIAL 50 FT. TIMED AND RAPID FIRE PISTOL TARGET

MATCH # *11*

RELAY # *2*

TARGET # *15*

STAGE # *2*

NONE OFFICIAL
WITHOUT THIS SEAL

AMERICAN TARGET CO.
1328 South Jason Street   Denver, Colorado 80223
LICENSE No. 5

**OFFICIAL
COMPETITION**
REGISTERED
U. S. PATENT OFFICE

B-3

A target used by Lu at an Iowa City shooting range
in the summer of 1991.

Dwight Nicholson, chairman of the physics department.

Jane Mechling Nicholson. *Courtesy of T. Scott Krenz.*

James Van Allen, father of the Space Age.

Shan in the official
university photograph
that was released to the
news media after the
killings.

Miya Rodolfo-Siosson, a
vivacious student activist
in happier times.

Prof. Bob Smith (*in striped shirt, on left*) and Prof. Chris Goertz.
Photo by Tom Jorgensen. © *University Relations Publications.*

Prof. Gerald L. Payne took over as chairman of a devastated physics
department. *Courtesy of T. Scott Krenz.*

Anne Cleary

Hundreds of people attend Anne Cleary's funeral at St. Patrick's Catholic Church in Iowa City. *Courtesy of AP. Published in "The Daily Iowan."*

Meeting the press the morning afterward: Ann Rhodes, vice president of university relations, and Hunter Rawlings, the university's president. *Courtesy of T. Scott Krenz.*

EIGHT

Reaching Out

They came to Iowa City in the 1970s. Both were married to other people at the time.

Erik Nilausen, a banker from Denmark, was married to a woman who studied art and jewelry design. Cheryl Tugwell was from eastern North Carolina. Having graduated from East Carolina University with a degree in elementary education, she came as the spouse of a University of Iowa graduate student.

After both marriages fell apart, Nilausen and Tugwell became neighbors by chance: They lived across Morningside Drive from one another in a pleasant neighborhood of neatly kept houses near Iowa City High School, on the east side of town. Both were outgoing by nature, and it wasn't long before they met and began living together.

In the mid-1980s, the couple signed up with Friends of International Students, volunteering to be a host family to a foreign student. "Basically, all you do is provide friendship," Tugwell said. "And Erik and I are interested in people."

The program encouraged host families to get together with their student once a month—but that was rarely possible, given the predictably busy schedules on both sides. In fact, Nilausen and Tugwell rarely saw the first student they were assigned, a married student from China. To begin with, he didn't have a telephone. And he virtually lived at the computer center, crunching data at all hours. His wife, a physician, was doing a residency in Mississippi, and he went to see her at every opportunity. But even the *single* Chinese students generally seemed to have far less time for social life than most other international students. "They just didn't party like the others—say, the South Americans," said Tugwell, who later served on the board of the Friends of International Students.

·In early 1988, Nilausen and Tugwell were paired with a second Chinese student, one who delighted them (and tried his best to see them on occasion) from the beginning. He was also a married man, although his wife had not yet joined him. Shan Linhua was friendly, cheerful, and—though brimming with self-confidence—soft-spoken. "Shan was very easy to talk to. And he was a very curious person, asking a lot of questions from our first meeting on," Tugwell recalled.

Shan had returned from China a few months earlier. He had gone home to marry Yang. Without being overbearing, Shan had seen to most of the details of their wedding from afar. It was a simple family-centered affair. But afterward, they held several festive celebrations, inviting friends from their undergraduate school, and even (in Shan's case) grade-school classmates from his ancestral village. Then Shan had to rush back to Iowa. All told, he had less than three weeks to spend in China. "We can have a honeymoon in Iowa City," he told Yang with a warm smile as he prepared to leave for the United States. "It's very nice there."

Shan had sought out a host family in large measure to ensure that Yang would have some extra support after she arrived later in the year. He was due for an extremely busy semester, and knew that he wouldn't be able to devote as much time as he'd have liked to help Yang get clued in and settled. Nilausen and Tugwell sensed all of this, but it hardly mattered to them. They were delighted that Shan had entered their lives—and, once they really got to know him, they were sure that they were also going to like Yang. In fact, they began looking forward to her arrival in August almost as much as Shan did.

From the start, Nilausen and Tugwell included Shan in many of their social activities, and especially their dinner parties, which usually included a cross-section of the community. Their parties almost always had a distinctly international flavor, from the food to the guests. And Shan fit right in. He talked openly and engagingly, he mingled, and he helped out in and around the kitchen.

Nilausen and Shan hit it off especially well. Both greatly enjoyed watching sports on TV, and loved to fish. They talked endlessly about fishing, but (with their busy schedules) they never did find a mutually convenient time to actually go fishing together. That didn't stop them, though, from rhapsodizing about the joys of the pastime.

Shan, a strong believer in reciprocating, that winter invited Nilausen and Tugwell to a Chinese New Year's party. When the couple arrived, Shan quickly left the dais (he was the emcee) to help Nilausen and Tugwell get settled; he introduced them all around. They were one of the few non-Chinese couples at the party. "We felt really honored," Tugwell recalled.

Several months after Yang arrived in Iowa City, Nilausen and Tugwell invited her and Shan to their traditional Christmas Eve dinner party. This was when Nilausen would spend the day in the kitchen, preparing a dinner of goose, red cabbage, candied sweet potatoes, and a rice dessert cooked in milk. Enough nationalities were represented that night to start a mini–United Nations, and Shan spent a good part of the evening talking world affairs and politics with a man from Germany, all the while nursing a glass of sweet red wine.

Shan loved a good glass or two of port. But one was all that he usually allowed himself—at least when Yang was around. This Nilausen quickly learned. At the Christmas Eve party, he approached Shan to offer a refill. But Yang quickly said something to Shan in Chinese, and he promptly and politely turned down Nilausen's offer. Whatever Yang said had been delivered in such an understated, even amusing, sort of way that the moment passed without awkwardness. Shan certainly didn't seem bothered. In fact, he broke into a broad grin.

The two couples, much to their mutual delight, discovered that they all were firstborns. They laughed and joked often about the supposed traits of their birthrights. Shan and Nilausen also shared much laughter about being married to "strong" women who didn't hesitate to speak their minds. With Yang, that quality wasn't as much in evidence, though; she was very discreet about it.

Like Nilausen, Shan fancied himself a chef. When he and Yang entertained Nilausen and Tugwell at their Parklawn apartment, Shan often did the cooking. Gradually he relinquished the cooking chores to Yang—but only after she had mastered his favorite dishes. Even then, he often hovered around the kitchen, looking over Yang's shoulder until she good-naturedly shooed him out of there.

Over many such dinners, Nilausen and Tugwell tried to get Shan to explain his line of research—but they never were able to get a good grip on what he said. It was far easier for Nilausen to detail the duties of a vice president for risk assessment at the Iowa State Bank and Trust Co., or for Tugwell to expound the theories of education, or for Yang to clarify the principles of electrical engineering. Finally, a frustrated Shan blurted out one evening "Space theory!" and left it at that. Everyone just laughed. "We never *did* understand," said Tugwell. "He never conveyed the importance of his work to us."

Neither did Shan speak much about his personal or family background. It wasn't as if he had something to hide; he just pretty much let others do the talking whenever the topic of conversation turned to people's roots. "All we knew was that his parents were farmers," Nilausen said.

At the end of one particular evening's gathering, Shan and Yang asked Nilausen and Tugwell to drop them off at Van Allen Hall on their way home. They wanted to go there to play computer video games. Van Allen Hall had become a multipurpose home away from home—a place to pass one's time in leisurely activities as well as to study physics and conduct experiments.

After a few months, largely due to new demands on their time, energy, and funds, the couples began to see less of one another. Yang found a job at the China Garden, a popular restaurant and bar in the adjacent community of Coralville. She worked six days a week, clearing tables, and saved almost every penny for her tuition. Tugwell, meantime, began doing graduate work at the university in education counseling, and now had classes on Wednesday—the one day of the week that Yang had off. "It became very hard for us to get together," Tugwell recalled. Nilausen added: "Although we didn't spend that much time together, we really felt very close."

Shan was also becoming increasingly preoccupied—not only with his research activities but also with the Chinese Students' Friendship Association. He was elected the group's president. Whenever someone needed help, whether it was a ride to the airport or help in moving, Shan was there—by then he and Yang had bought a shiny new Honda Accord, their one splurge. But Shan got it for a good price. "He was a good negotiator and I'm sure he got his way," Nilausen said.

Shan became busier for yet another reason: He had found God. Earlier in the fall, the Rev. Tom Miller had run into C.M. at the annual potluck dinner, and he was delighted to learn that C.M. had two roommates, also from China, at his Dubuque Street apartment. One Saturday morning shortly after that, Miller made a point of introducing himself to both Lu and Shan. But where Lu was dismissive, unrelentingly questioning and challenging Miller, to the point of making the others squirm, Shan became a regular member of the Saturday morning group, bringing a genuine curiosity to the subject. After the grocery-shopping excursion to Econofoods, he participated in the Bible-study fellowship group as much as anyone else, displaying a deep interest in the discussions.

"It was clear-cut from the beginning: Shan Linhua was easygoing and very likable. He had a personality that everyone liked, especially the girls. But Lu Gang was gruff, not as likable. Whereas Shan fit in easily, Lu did not," Miller recalled. "So there were a whole lot of reasons why Lu didn't like Shan. Also, Lu never received Christ into his life, as Shan later did. I see it as a Cain and Abel story— Cain killed his brother over jealousy. Shan and Lu became a modern-day version of that."

Miller came to view Shan not only as a potential convert to Christianity but as a genuine friend. Soon the Saturday morning ritual became one that Miller truly looked forward to, and not just another part of his job.

When the weather finally turned pleasant, the students often piled into Miller's van and went out for pizza. One summer day, the minister drove them clear to Muscatine for a day of picnicking and speed-boating on the Mississippi River. "There was real friendship," Miller recalled.

And when Shan or any of the others needed clothes, Miller took him or her to the Budget Shop, a secondhand clothing store on Riverside Drive. It was there that Shan shopped for a sports jacket for a very special occasion. The first he tried on was a green double-knit that was much too loud. "Tom, how do I look?" Shan asked with an innocent smile. Miller took one look at the garish garment and suggested that Shan keep looking. Shan did, eventually settling on a tweed that was nicely cut—even if it was half a size too big.

Not long after that shopping trip, Shan wore the old-but-new jacket proudly to the campus Bible fellowship's annual banquet. It was there that he stood up and announced that he had decided to become a Christian.

* * *

The contrast between Shan's exuberant embrace of life all around him and Lu's isolation and alienation seemed starkest when the two were together. Some of the reasons for this may be seen in Lu's behavior.

Even when Lu found himself surrounded by others, whether at a Chinese students' dinner party or involved in some physics department function, he projected an aloofness that put a certain gulf between himself and others.

When a large and happy group of Chinese students went to a dance celebrating the Chinese New Year, Lu tagged along. But after they got to the club, Lu just sat at the bar alone, nursing a pitcher of Bud Lite while the others danced the night away.

Lu also joined in when another group drove to Davenport one Sunday for a day's outing at Wacky Waters, an amusement park. But, even after making the sixty-mile trip and paying the $7 admissions fee, Lu never got on one ride. "He just stood there watching everybody else," recalled C.M., shaking his head in bafflement.

Every year, the physics department held two big social events—a spring picnic and a Christmas party. But throughout the year there were plenty of smaller gatherings, including regular dinner parties hosted by faculty members. And Lu showed up at many such functions. But, again, he usually ended up in a corner by himself.

One Thanksgiving, Robert Alan Smith, a popular new physics professor, invited a group of foreign students to his home for dinner. Among them were Lu Gang, Shan Linhua, and Yang Yiling. At one point during the evening, Lu began telling Yang about why he had recently broken up with a girlfriend. Yang was genuinely surprised, since if Lu had a steady girlfriend, she was the best-kept secret in town.

Lu tried to impress others as well, talking boastfully about all the friends he supposedly had at the Sports Column—"my favorite public place in Iowa City," he often said. According to Lu, he had made so many friends among the coeds there that he was also beginning to make enemies among the male competition. Since no other Chinese student patronized the Sports Column, Lu knew that no one could challenge or doubt his word. In fact, they began to laugh at him—behind his back. Some even felt sorry for him.

And Lu didn't stop there. He soon began talking openly (not so much with outright braggadocio as with a stiff casualness) about his many "liaisons," as he put it, with both Chinese and American women, including married ones. He also claimed that he had begun sleeping with girls while he was still in high school. What Lu conveniently did not disclose was the sad truth: He was so desperate for female companionship that he was taking out anonymous personal ads in the newspapers.

Still, Lu ineptly pushed on. One New Year's Day, An Tao and a roommate asked Lu for a ride across town to the apartment of two Chinese coeds who had recently arrived at the university. Lu readily acquiesced. Arriving at the girls' apartment, Lu also went inside, where the group played cards, ate, and chatted about life in Iowa. Lu didn't contribute much to the conversation that day. But several nights later he returned to the girls' apartment—alone, uninvited, and unannounced—with an awkward, nerdy smile on his face. Spooked, the girls told him they were busy, and closed the door.

Lu gave his classmates yet other reasons to laugh at him. Many of the Chinese students congregated at noontime in the canteen of Van Allen Hall and used its microwave oven to warm their lunches brought from home. One day the topic of conversation turned to the case of a University of Iowa medical school professor, a Chinese woman, who had filed a sexual discrimination lawsuit against the university and several of her male colleagues.

Lu suddenly launched into a tirade about "dirty" university officials and ranted about how the "little guys" needed to arm themselves in order to protect their rights against "bad guys" who were only interested in oppressing others and "covering their own asses." Didn't they know that the right to bear arms was what allowed the American civil-rights activists to finally secure their constitutional rights? If they hadn't gone into the South so heavily armed, Lu said, they would have been defenseless.

D.Y., one of the Chinese students, almost choked on his noodles. Laughing, he looked up and told Lu that he must be watching too many Clint Eastwood movies. Which was true. Everybody in the lunchroom howled. Lu stopped coming to the canteen for lunch. He went home to eat by himself.

"That Lu Gang," Shan finally snapped one day. "You can't listen to him. What does he know?" But there was *one* thing that Shan and Lu *did* agree on: Their academic supervisor, Chris Goertz, might be a top scholar and a world-renowned researchers, but he was also one excessively demanding taskmaster. And therefore neither Shan nor Lu especially cared much for him as a person.

NINE

Gathering Clouds

In the old days, things were a lot easier. Even by the late 1970s affirmative action, diversity in the workplace, and multiculturalism were alien concepts to all but the most socially aware. So, as chairman of the Department of Physics and Astronomy, James Van Allen could hire just about anybody he wanted to. In 1973, after he heard Christoph Klaus Goertz give a seminar, Van Allen knew that the twenty-seven-year-old theoretical space physicist would be a splendid addition to the University of Iowa.

Goertz, who had just earned a Ph.D. at Rhodes University in Grahamstown, South Africa, had been invited to Iowa City to speak about his field of expertise, which ranged from the aurora borealis (the Northern Lights) to the magnetic fields of Earth, Saturn, and Jupiter.

After the well-attended seminar, the low-keyed Van Allen approached Goertz and, on the spot, offered him a job as a postdoctoral research associate. "In those days, you could do that," Van Allen said. Goertz proved equally decisive in accepting the surprise offer. "It was almost immediate—both ways," Van Allen recalled.

Goertz, who had been a lecturer at Rhodes University,

arrived at the University of Iowa in the fall of 1973. Almost immediately, Van Allen invited him to participate in a research project. That December, Pioneer 10 was due for a close encounter with Jupiter, and aboard the spacecraft were many of Van Allen's research instruments. Goertz was elated to have the chance to work with Van Allen, truly a giant in his field.

Some historians say that the race to outer space can be traced to an after-dinner conversation one spring evening in 1950, in Van Allen's modest brick home in Silver Spring, Maryland. There, Van Allen led a spirited discussion among a small but influential group of scientists that culminated in the declaration of an International Geophysical Year (IGY) designed to bring together the world's top stargazers, who would share research data and critique one another's exploration strategies.

It was partly in that competitive spirit that President Dwight D. Eisenhower declared that the United States would launch a "small, unnamed earth-circling satellite" as a part of its participation in the IGY. The Soviets countered the next day with an announcement that they would launch their own satellite—and, of course, eventually beat the United States to it by successfully launching Sputnik I.

It was also Van Allen who rescued at least a portion of the national honor shortly afterward by discovering the deadly radiation belts that surround Earth—an achievement that landed the unassuming scientist on the cover of *Time* Magazine.

A native Iowan, Van Allen became an avid reader of things scientific and technical while still a child, and once built a coil which sent out foot-long electrical charges that made his hair stand on end. During World War II, he played a key role in one of the war effort's most closely guarded secret programs: the development of a state-of-the-art fuse to increase the accuracy and effectiveness of bombs, rockets, and mortar shells. Van Allen traveled all over the world testing such devices, which proved a resounding success and were widely considered among the top scientific achievements of the war.

After the war, Van Allen again turned his attention to space. And by 1950, he returned to the University of Iowa (which had awarded him a Ph.D. in 1939) to head up its physics department.

*   *   *

Goertz was an internationally recognized leader in the study of the complex properties of ionized gases, or plasma, the so-called fourth state of matter—the other three being solids, fluids, and neutral gases. "But it is estimated that over 99 percent of matter in the universe is in the form of plasmas," Van Allen explained. Plasma physics also is an essential ingredient in the ongoing efforts to produce electrical power through nuclear fusion.

Unlike Van Allen, who is an experimental observationist, Goertz was primarily a theoretician. Practitioners in each field often had trouble communicating with one another. "Most theorists are just sort of floating, way out there," Van Allen said, chuckling. But Goertz was different. He had an intuitive ability to grasp experimental data, and Van Allen was quick to recognize that.

The two ended up collaborating on some of the department's forty-plus U.S. space missions, ranging from satellites of the Earth and the Moon to the first-ever flights past a comet, an asteroid, and Venus, Mars, Jupiter, Saturn, Uranus, and Neptune. "He was very facile with math and physical theory, and unfailingly came up with astute observations," Van Allen said. "He became one of my favorite collaborators."

Within a year, Goertz was named a visiting professor—and placed on the tenure track. He and Van Allen also began jointly teaching a physics class. "Chris was also a very good teacher," Van Allen recalled. He felt that Goertz had a way of engaging the students that made them eager to learn.

Goertz's early years at the university were marked by intense collaboration with Van Allen. They met every day, poring over their rapidly accumulating data as the space-exploration community awaited their latest findings. To this day, data from Pioneer 10 and Pioneer 11 form a central part of Van Allen's research existence.

Pioneer 10 made the first-ever encounter with Jupiter in December 1973, yielding a vast quantity of knowledge about its magnetosphere. Pioneer 11 encountered Jupiter a year later, and—though on a different trajectory—confirmed and substantially expanded upon the earlier findings. Almost every piece of information sent back by the Pioneers was new, and worthy of publication in the leading space journals of the day. "It was an exceedingly exciting time," Van Allen recalled.

In 1979, Pioneer 11 passed Saturn. The data it returned to Earth from that planet, with its beautiful and mysterious system of rings and satellites, provided enough fodder to occupy Van Allen and Goertz for another full year. After that, as both Pioneers continued on their remarkable journeys that would eventually take them out of the solar system, the two men's research interests began to diverge, and their collaborative work to wane. (Although Goertz and Van Allen had worked closely together, they were never close socially. But that was not surprising, given their 30-year age difference.)

In 1981, as Lu Gang was just beginning college in China, Goertz won appointment as a full professor at the university. He had become an internationally recognized leader in plasma physics and an expert on Jupiter's moons. Having earned his bachelor's degree from the Technische Universitat in Berlin, Germany, he also did short stints as a visiting scientist at the Max Planck Institute for Extraterrestrial Physics in Garching, Germany, and at the Massachusetts Institute of Technology in Cambridge. Eventually he would author more than 150 scientific articles in professional journals.

Goertz also served as editor of the *Journal of Geophysical Research—Space Physics*, the foremost magazine-format publication in the field. Each issue carried as many as forty articles. But before a research paper can be published, it must be reviewed by the author's peers. As editor, it was Goertz's job to farm out the articles to "referees" around the country. This task required the juggling skills of a traffic cop, the salesmanship of a car dealer, and the tact of a diplomat. Also, Goertz had to know who the experts were in each and every arcane corner of space physics—the prospective judges.

It wasn't always easy to persuade busy researchers to take time out to review a colleague's paper; the job of a peer reviewer wasn't exactly glamorous—and it didn't pay. Too, even after someone had agreed to review a paper, Goertz had to stay on top of him or her to make sure that they both met their deadlines. And each paper required at least two judges.

It also was Goertz's responsibility to judge the judges, evaluating their opinions to make sure that they had been not only accurate but fair. After all, in such a small and highly competitive field, one's colleague also was one's rival. It wasn't unknown for a researcher, given the chance, to anonymously trash another's work out of envy and competition. But, more often than not, the reviewers raised serious and legitimate questions—and when that happened, it was Goertz's job to relay them to the paper's author for replies. Ultimately, it was Goertz's decision whether or not to publish a research paper. (As editor, he also could solicit papers on certain topics of special interest.)

All this Goertz did during his "free" time, which typically came at the end of a regular workday. As Van

Allen Hall began to thin out for the night, Goertz would finally turn away from a chalkboard filled with seemingly indecipherable mathematical equations, pour himself a fresh cup of coffee, light another cigarette, and then pull out a stack of manuscripts, to settle in for a few hours of work as editor.

The demands of teaching, doing world-class research, supervising Ph.D. candidates, and editing a top science journal required one to be highly organized—and Goertz was efficiency personified. Somehow he also found time to become active in many professional organizations, serving as a member of the European Space Foundation, the Committee on the Future of Geophysics in Europe, and NASA's Space and Earth Science Advisory Committee on the scientific uses of the Space Station. It was more than obvious that hiring Goertz was one of the best personnel decisions that Van Allen had ever made.

Like so many other people who came to the university, Goertz grew to love Iowa. Van Allen could recall only once when Goertz talked even vaguely of returning to his native Germany. "He often expressed his pleasure at being here, though not in a sentimental sense," Van Allen said.

Goertz had many interests beyond physics. He read widely, and was an engaging conversationist—whether the topic was politics, art, nature, cooking, wine, or the state of America's public education system. Although he loved to travel, he took pride in having become something of an expert on the charms of Iowa City. He especially enjoyed showing the local sights to visitors and newcomers. (One of his favorite spots was Hickory Hill Park, a heavily wooded preserve full of hiking trails.) "He wanted to help me see all the aspects of Iowa City that he found beautiful," recalled Usha Mallik, an associate professor of physics and astronomy.

Mallick described Goertz as a man who was "always thinking," adding: "He really wanted excellence—from himself and from everyone else." According to Mallick, Goertz was a person who could "enliven the conversation at any party because he always liked to stir up the discussion."

That was a quality which Jo Ann Beard also admired in Goertz. She was a graduate student working her way through school as managing editor of the *Journal of Geophysical Research—Space Physics*. Beard, who was studying nonfiction writing, had little understanding of science, but Goertz often took time out to try to explain physics to her. Once he patiently tried to get across to her the notion of dimensions, using as an example an ant that he spotted one late afternoon crawling across the office floor. Another time, Beard ruefully confessed her inability to comprehend the concept of infinity. "Who *can*?" Goertz asked rhetorically.

Goertz was equally giving of his time with students. "He was always there for you whenever you had a problem," recalled Maygol Sarvi, a biochemistry major. "He would meet with you after class and was willing to do whatever he could to help," she said. Sarvi, who graduated in 1991, said Goertz was not only a talented teacher who could clearly articulate a complicated concept, but also an extremely personable professor. "He was certainly one of the finest men I knew—a real gentleman in the true sense of the word," she added.

But not all the physics students held Goertz in such high regard, and that was especially true among the graduate research assistants who had much closer dealings with Goertz than did the more impressionable undergraduates.

Goertz, although considered humorless, was certainly not an unfriendly man—but he did not suffer fools gladly. When it came to theoretical space physics, he could toss out ideas faster than others could digest them. "Chris had a very, very fertile intellect," said John Lyons, a physicist who worked in the plasma research group that Goertz headed. And he drove his graduate students relentlessly. "Chris was the sort of person who demanded the best of himself and demanded the best of others," said Lyons. "If you weren't brilliant, that was okay. But if you were just dogging it, that wasn't okay."

In time, Goertz began to feel that Lu, though a brilliant student, wasn't working hard enough—so he began pushing him. The turning point in their relationship was their Paris trip in the summer of 1987 to attend an international physics conference. Goertz became annoyed when Lu decided to spend most of that summer traveling in Western Europe after the Paris conference, instead of going directly back to work in Iowa.

The estrangement took a more serious turn that fall, with the arrival of Shan Linhua from Texas A&M. It was only then that Lu's rarefied status as the department's top graduate student began to erode. In the qualifying examinations for the Ph.D. program in physics, Lu had made the highest score at the university. But when Shan took his examination two years later, his score was even higher. In a class they took together on general relativity, Lu got an A minus. Shan got an A.

Shan Linhua, the new kid on the block, was outshining Lu—and in the process was replacing him as Goertz's favorite student. Goertz, himself a department superstar who was bringing in more than $500,000 in NASA grants, supervised both Lu and Shan. And there was no question in Goertz's mind that Shan worked harder than Lu; he put in longer hours, and otherwise applied himself in a way that Lu did not. Shan also was more open to suggestions from Goertz as well as other professors. And, unlike Lu, he was neither aloof nor arrogant.

Lu, on the other hand, became increasingly distracted and less motivated. "I'd say Chris probably felt that Lu Gang wasn't working as hard as he might," Lyons recalled.

In such situations, other faculty members said, Goertz could be extremely tough on a student. And as he piled on the work, Lu complained bitterly that Goertz was being particularly unfair to him—and was exploiting his research assistants in general.

The difference in the quality of work between Lu and Shan was exemplified by their Ph.D. dissertations. Lu's was rather mundane, dealing with the behavior and properties of certain gases in space when electrically charged. Shan's thesis focused on the rings of Saturn—a far more compelling and relevant subject. Shan's dissertation, according to several professors familiar with both papers, was simply a better piece of scientific work. "Lu Gang was a very good student," said Lyons, "but he didn't seem to have quite the sufficient insight into how things worked to really guide his own research as much as you'd like."

In time, Goertz's favoritism toward Shan became clear to many others in the department besides Lu. And it was one that Shan seemed to nurture. He made a point of frequently soliciting Goertz for suggestions and advice. The two also published numerous joint papers in the journals. Many evenings, Shan was late for dinner because he had lingered in Van Allen Hall to consult with Goertz.

Under Goertz's tutelage, Shan flourished. But he also secretly shared Lu's dislike for Goertz as a person, viewing the professor as domineering and sometimes even brusque. "Chris can be very firm. He's very German that way," conceded one of Goertz's colleagues on the physics faculty. "But he was also fair and you could reason with him. There were times when Chris did find weak points in Lu's work and he indicated that Lu should go back and fix them up. But I didn't see any particular harshness in Chris's handling of Lu."

In the summer of 1990 there was a colloquium at the department, attended by nine students—Lu Gang included. Many of them talked in some detail about their research. When Lu's turn came, recalled Don Johnson, an Illinois State University physics graduate who was about to begin a research assistantship at Iowa, "I couldn't really understand what he was relaying because of the fact that he didn't know very much English at all." But what really struck Johnson was the way Goertz seemed to take out after Lu when Lu finished.

Goertz, Johnson recalled, "immediately started asking him questions about his research. But Lu Gang didn't seem to understand what he was being asked, and didn't know how to answer. And you could just tell that he kind of felt like he was on the spot and he was very tense." The tension between Goertz and Lu was palpable, and the strain between the two clearly was one that had been building for some time.

"Both Lu and Shan were pressured by Goertz, but that's his style," said another graduate student. "Maybe if he had been a little easier on them, Lu and Shan might have had a different, less competitive relationship."

Unlike the hotheaded Lu, Shan did not go around bad-mouthing Goertz. He confided his true feelings only over pillow talk with Yang Yiling, his wife. Shan was wise and coolheaded enough to keep his eyes on the prize and not let his personal feelings sidetrack him from earning a Ph.D.

Lu, who was immensely proud of himself and had an ego to match, began criticizing Goertz endlessly—almost obsessively. Lu became so disgruntled that he absented himself from Van Allen Hall more and more frequently, staying home instead to watch the afternoon soap operas and renting Clint Eastwood videos to pass the night away. His prolonged, unexplained absences were quickly noticed throughout the department.

As a result, Goertz began piling even more work on Lu—and also started dropping in on room 513 in Van Allen Hall, conducting spotchecks on his fading star student. This treatment humiliated Lu—but he nevertheless decided to rise to the challenge. He put everything else out of his life: no more dinners out, no more nights at the Sports Column, no more trips to the bowling alley, no more video movies at home.

Lu also began virtually living at Van Allen Hall. In the morning, he was the first one there. At night, he was the last to leave—sometimes not until well after midnight. No one spent more time there than Lu. He spoke hardly at all to his fellow students, focusing intently on his work as if he had blinders on. "Lu was pretty deadpan most of that time," recalled Lyons. Indeed, Lu did a masterful job of keeping his rage hidden from view.

One day, when Lu came up with an unexpected conclusion and took it to Goertz, the professor responded by sternly questioning him, as if there was no doubt that Lu had made a mistake. That made Lu livid. The meeting ended badly, with Goertz remarking that Lu was perhaps spending too much time on the computer, running up the bill. Lu became even more outraged when his conclusion proved correct after all. It was Goertz who had made the mistake.

Suffering one perceived indignity after another, Lu began to despise Goertz, and railed about his thesis adviser to anyone who would listen. Despite whatever fantasies he harbored about being a lone cowboy taking on a group of evil oppressors, Lu realized that the odds were heavily stacked against him, and that he therefore might have to take extraordinary action to protect himself.

"Usually, an individual is too weak, both politically and financially, to oppose a giant organization," Lu said. But there were exceptions. Just consider the case of Dr. Jean Y. Jew, he urged a friend. Jew, 41, was a Chinese-American professor of anatomy who had recently won a highly publicized sexual harassment lawsuit against the University of Iowa and several of her male colleagues in the

College of Medicine's anatomy department. There were lessons to be learned from Dr. Jew's case, Lu said.

Jew had arrived at the university in 1973 as a postgraduate associate in the medical school. Then only twenty-four, she had earned her medical degree at Tulane University, where she studied under Dr. Terence Williams, the anatomy department chairman. After Williams accepted an offer to chair the University of Iowa's anatomy department, he brought with him three other physicians from Tulane's medical school, including Jew. The other two were men.

A year after her arrival in Iowa, Jew received a faculty appointment as an assistant professor. In 1979, she was granted tenure and was promoted to associate professor. But Williams's arrival in Iowa City created an uproar in the medical school's anatomy department. Many faculty members deeply resented the newcomers. Among the former was Dr. Nicholas Halmi, who was one of the department's most senior individuals. Prior to 1973, he had held a top administrative post in the department.

Almost from day one, Halmi and several colleagues began spreading scurrilous rumors about Williams and Jew, alleging that she had secured her position by providing sexual favors to Williams. At various times between 1973 and 1980, cartoons were posted on the door and wall outside Halmi's laboratory, depicting Jew and Williams in sexually suggestive poses.

Another Jew and Williams detractor, Dr. Robert Tamanek, joined in, initiating numerous conversations about the two with other faculty members, staffers, and even graduate students. He kept that up for thirteen years.

A third faculty member, Dr. William Kaelber, in a drunken outburst in January of 1979, hurled epithets at Jew as she walked down a corridor in the department, calling her a "slut," "bitch," and "whore." Four years later,

Kaelber again publicly referred to Jew as a "whore," this time in the presence of another senior faculty member as they were about to begin an evaluation of Jew for promotion to full professor. At the same time, a salacious limerick was scrawled in the department's men's room, insinuating a sexual relationship between Jew and Williams.

Jew was denied the promotion. Then, in that same year (1983), Williams stepped down as chairman—and, under the new department head, the harassment of Jew at last subsided.

It was shortly after the 1979 incident involving Kaelber that Jew filed a written sexual harassment complaint with Dr. John W. Eckstein, dean of the College of Medicine. But Eckstein and university vice president May Brodbeck advised Jew, in a face-to-face meeting, that nothing could be done—saying that a single woman sometimes just had to live with these kinds of problems, especially in the small-town fishbowl environment that was Iowa City.

Jew finally filed a sexual harassment lawsuit in federal court. It took seven years to adjudicate, but in August of 1990 a U.S. District Court judge in Des Moines ruled against the university. In a scathing, thirty-four-page opinion, Judge Harold Vietor ordered the university to promote Jew to the position of full professor, with commensurate pay retroactive to 1984. The university ultimately paid Jew $176,000 in damages and back pay, and her lawyer $895,000 in legal fees and expenses.

Lu was transfixed by the case and talked incessantly about it. Dr. Jew's triumph was a "really rare" example of good winning out over evil, Lu said, claiming that Jew owed her success in court largely to her high income, which enabled her to afford the services of a private attorney. On the other hand, the university was represented by the Iowa attorney general's office—at taxpayer expense. That, Lu concluded, was just one more example of how the system is stacked against an individual.

Even more outrageous was the university's flat-out refusal to recognize Jew's initial complaints, much less do anything to correct the problem. Worst of all, however, was the way that cowardly administrators conducted themselves, Lu concluded. They issued a public apology to Jew only after the judge rendered his denunciatory decision! The lesson of the case, Lu said, was that Jew's victory over the establishment was, sadly, an aberration.

"There exists no justice for little people in this world," Lu said. "Extraordinary action has to be taken to preserve this world as a better place to live."

In the end, Jew's case proved only one thing to Lu: Without an equalizer, "little guys" like himself had no chance when fighting the power elite. Mistakenly recalling that American civil-rights activists had armed themselves during the 1960s for the struggle, Lu concluded that he too might have to turn to guns. "They make it possible for an individual to fight against the Mafia or dirty university officials," said Lu.

TEN

A Miscalculation

In December 1990, Shan Linhua was awarded his Ph.D. This academic milestone came as a shattering blow to Lu Gang. At 26 Shan was a year younger than Lu. He also had been at the University of Iowa a year less, having transferred from Texas A&M. And yet, he had now beaten Lu across the finish line. Moreover, Shan finished with a perfect 4.0 grade point average; Lu's was 3.84.

All this caused Lu to lose face, and for that he blamed not himself but Chris Goertz, his and Shan's adviser. Lu seethed at Goertz's blatant favoritism of Shan. But what could Lu do? He was a powerless foreign graduate student at the mercy of a system that was biased against minorities. To get along, you had to kowtow to the Chris Goertzes of the world. Look at Jean Jew: Even she, a highly paid, well-educated doctor, was all but helpless in the face of merciless—and very public—harassment. And she silently endured the appalling indignities for years before fighting back. If they continued to treat him so shabbily, Lu vowed, they would be in for a big surprise. Not all Asians were meek.

Lu wasn't scheduled to get his degree until the following May, so in late 1990, while still completing his thesis, he decided to get a jump on job-hunting. But again he was stymied by a major obstacle: In applying for a job, a letter of recommendation from one's academic adviser was clearly in order. But Lu's relationship with Goertz had deteriorated to the point where he was convinced that a letter from Goertz would be more a hindrance than a help. So Lu turned instead to Dwight Nicholson, chairman of the physics department.

Lu had taken a class several years earlier with Nicholson and found him to be easygoing and quite approachable. The door to his second-floor office, next to a busy stairwell, was always open. And it was widely known that Nicholson was especially accommodating to foreign students. Every winter, he would lead an expedition of newly arrived foreign students who were unfamiliar with American blizzards, taking them down by the Iowa River to teach them how to walk up and down the steep hills covered with ice or snow. It was as much an excuse for a fun outing as anything else. But that was Nicholson.

Underneath that gregarious facade, however, Nicholson was a diligent, hardworking man who had a tendency to keep things to himself. As chairman, he was determined to shield everyone else from all the problems and distractions that come with running a department with hundreds of faculty members, research scientists, postdoctoral fellows, students, and staffers. When hard times hit the nation's science community and funds began to dry up, Nicholson quietly offered to take a pay cut in hopes of helping to avert any layoffs in the department. He didn't tell Jane, his wife, about that.

Nicholson was both discreet and sensitive by nature, but circumstances also conspired to reinforce those traits. Most of the time, he lived by himself in a large house, just north of the campus, that he and Jane owned. They had a commuting marriage: Jane, a Ph.D. in French literature, taught at the University of Tulsa in Oklahoma.

Neither person liked being apart (they had been living that way for six years) and did everything possible to make their arrangement work. They took turns visiting one another, as often as every other weekend, making sure that their hours together would be "quality time." And every night, without fail, they talked on the telephone.

Because he was alone much of the time, Nicholson didn't mind—as he might have otherwise—putting in brutally long hours at the office. He had not set out to become chairman when James Van Allen retired in 1985, but he was secretly pleased to accept when the job was offered to him, virtually by popular acclaim. Twice more thereafter, at three-year intervals, Nicholson was reelected to the post. He saw his job as something of a public service, so worked assiduously at carrying out his responsibilities.

Dwight Nicholson and Jane Mechling, both natives of Wisconsin, were high school sweethearts. Dwight was the son of Wisconsin hog and grain farmers who never even made it to high school. The senior Nicholsons lived in Racine, a city aside Lake Michigan, just south of Milwaukee. Jane also grew up in southern Wisconsin, in the inland town of Beloit. Her father was a farm machinery purchasing agent, her mother a public school secretary. The Mechlings moved to Racine when she was sixteen. At Horlick High School, Jane ended up sitting in home room right behind Dwight, a strapping, handsome young man with a fascination for physics and chemistry.

Together, the pair attended the University of Wisconsin, he majoring in physics and she in French and Spanish. In 1969, they got married in Racine just a week after graduation, timing their wedding to attract their college friends before everyone left Wisconsin (perhaps for good). That fall, they moved to Berkeley, where he enrolled at the University of California as a doctoral candidate.

With the exception of a year of dual studies in Paris, the Nicholsons stayed in northern California until 1975, when Dwight was awarded his Ph.D. in plasma physics. Then they moved to the University of Colorado in Boulder, where Jane had been accepted as a master's student in comparative literature. "Long ago, we each decided on an academic career," said Jane. And now that they had become the quintessential two-career academic couple, there would be no time for children.

It was Dwight's turn to tag along—but, inactivity not being part of his code, either, he became a postdoctoral research associate and lecturer in the university's department of astrogeophysics. In fact, he also wrote what became a highly regarded graduate-level textbook, *Introduction to Plasma Theory*, working on it every night for nearly three years. Published in 1983, it is still widely used.

They arrived in Iowa City in 1978, happy to be back in the Midwest—though Jane had some initial misgivings, preferring Wisconsin and its more progressive tradition. Dwight quickly helped her to fall in love with the gentle charm of their new location, however. "He was a country boy at heart," Johanna Nicholson, Dwight's seventy-year-old mother, told a reporter for the Racine *Journal Times*. Though his work took him all over the world, she said, "He couldn't wait to get back to Iowa City. He loved it there."

Nicholson arrived at the university as an assistant professor. Jane enrolled there as a doctoral student in comparative literature. In 1984, after completing all her degree requirements but for her thesis defense, she got a job at Oregon State University in Corvallis, teaching French and French literature for a year. That marked the start of their commuting marriage, something that he found more difficult to accept than she did. As the time approached for her to head West, there was real pain in his eyes. It was only then that Jane realized just how hard her departure was going to be for him. But she was committed. "It was a new opportunity for me to have a career," Jane said.

They talked nightly by phone, and saw one another at least once a month. It wasn't easy, but by then they had been married for 15 years—"a solid base," in Jane's words. "There was never a moment when either one of us felt this couldn't go on," she recalled.

In 1985, the couple had special reason to celebrate: She was awarded her Ph.D., and he was named chairman of the physics department. But their happiness was bittersweet—because in the fall Jane moved to Tulsa, where she had been hired by the University of Tulsa as an assistant professor specializing in the nineteenth-century French novel.

Around the University of Iowa campus, Dwight Nicholson was a popular figure out of class as well as in. Nearly every day—come rain, snow, or sleet—he could be seen leisurely pedaling his bicycle between Van Allen Hall and his home on Kimball Road. In bad weather, this practical physics professor simply used snow tires on his bike.

Though he was an academic scientist and university administrator through and through, Nicholson was not content solely with an ivory-tower existence. He cared deeply about both the general environment and the community in which he lived. And he made sure that the university got involved in local issues, often telephoning Hunter R. Rawlings III, the university's president, to offer his opinions on a variety of public issues—along with suggestions on what stance the university might take on a particular issue. "It was always interesting to hear from Dwight. He was a real campus citizen," Rawlings said. "He didn't want this to be a place that was isolated from the rest of the community."

Nicholson also was popular as a lecturer. He had the special knack of making his classes interesting, and didn't talk down to his students. He also tried to stay in touch with many of them even after they left Iowa—keeping tabs on their careers, and continuing to offer them encouragement and counsel.

"He had very good relations with students," recalled his predecessor, James Van Allen. He operated characteristically with the door of his office open throughout the day, and often into the evening, and on weekends. "He was a special friend of the Chinese students," added Van Allen. "He went out of his way to give them every consideration." An Tao agreed: "Dr. Nicholson was a very good guy. He was like a friend. Whenever you needed help, his door was open. You never needed an appointment with him."

* * *

When Lu Gang walked into Nicholson's office, the chairman was predictably amiable. But when Lu asked him for a letter of recommendation, the administrator balked.

"What about Professor Goertz? Have you asked him?" he inquired.

Lu hadn't anticipated that response, knowing full well that Nicholson was aware of his difficulties with Goertz.

"Nuh-no," Lu stammered.

"Well, you'd better ask him first," Nicholson said with a smile that signaled an end to the conversation.

Lu, seemingly accepting Nicholson's reply gracefully, nodded and quickly left. However, as he was walking home, his anger began to grow with each step. Never had he felt more boxed in: He certainly couldn't bring himself to ask Goertz for a letter of recommendation; he'd had it with going to *that* guy with hat in hand. Enough was enough! So, Lu vowed to find a job without any help from Goertz. Jobs, after all, were plentiful.

Or were they? In fact, a glut of candidates for positions was developing. Joblessness in physics, for example, was at its highest in twenty years. And young scientists and engineers fortunate enough to find work couldn't command much more than $18,000 to $25,000 a year. According to the American Institute of Physics, even the most talented young physicists were having trouble finding jobs—and this was true across all branches of physics, from high-energy particle physics to plasma physics. As many as 66 percent of the 1991 graduates in astrophysics could do no better than land postdoctoral fellowships, which are slots intended to be something of an academic hiatus between jobs. And many of them bounced from one such fellowship to another.

Public funds also became especially tight as the U.S. federal budget deficit worsened during the Reagan years. And the hardest hit because of that were researchers engaged in seemingly esoteric endeavors that had not readily identifiable short-term payoff. Even established scientists like Chris Goertz could no longer assume a steady funding stream.

Inevitably, questions of which research avenues to fund and which to abandon became politicized as never before. And the winners, increasingly, were not necessarily those with the most meritorious ideas, but rather those most adept at promoting themselves—in Washington and through the often uncritical news media. At the same time, funds for individual researchers were being severely drained by an unprecedented array of Big Science projects—most notably the planned orbiting space station; a colossal, underground atom-smasher in Texas; the Hubble Space Telescope; and the drive to map the entire human genetic code.

Getting grants—which meant jobs for young researchers—was becoming a crapshoot.

Nicholson knew that Lu's job search would not be easy. After Lu left his office, Nicholson went to see Goertz, and recounted his conversation with Lu Gang. Goertz was chagrined. True, relations could be better between himself and Lu, but they were certainly not so bad as Lu had evidently assumed. Goertz promptly sought out Lu, and graciously—but insistently—offered to write him one or more letters of recommendation. As many as he needed, Goertz insisted.

Begrudgingly, Lu took Goertz up on his offer. But that led to even more hard feelings on Lu's part when for some reason several of Goertz's letters missed their deadline. This kind of slippage, Lu became convinced, was the primary reason that he was still jobless.

When spring arrived, Lu temporarily set aside his job search and concentrated on his upcoming oral examination—a grueling exercise that amounts to a defense of one's doctoral thesis before a group of professors sitting like a panel of doubting Thomases. This would be Lu's final hurdle before getting his doctoral degree. And he was fairly bursting with confidence.

The title of Lu's thesis was "A Study of the Critical Ionization Velocity Effect by Particle-in-Cell Simulation." It was a theoretical interpretation of certain plasma phenomena having to do with the interaction of specific gases in space when electrically charged. To some scientists, the CIV mechanism was a possible explanation for the formation of the early solar system—but the mechanism had not been sufficiently demonstrated in space experiments. And it was Lu's supposition that the CIV mechanism might be more complicated than thought to be.

Lu set out to test his theory by designing, under Goertz's supervision, a series of mathematically based computer simulations of a neutral gas moving across magnetized plasma. The results ended up shedding *some* light on the efficiency of the CIV mechanism under certain circumstances. But it was hardly the stuff of Nobel Prizes.

On a Sunday afternoon, April 21, the day before his scheduled oral examination, Lu happily went shopping for party foods, stopping at Chong's Supermarket and East–West Oriental Foods, both just around the corner from his apartment. He planned to throw a little party afterward, to celebrate.

And why not? Lu had taken the time to review with Goertz every detail of his upcoming defense, going over each procedure, leaving out nothing that might be expected of him on April 22. Goertz would be among the five-member examination committee, and Lu secretly fretted over that, fearful that this demanding professor would be excessively tough on him. But there was nothing Lu could do about it, and so he tried to banish the thought. Maybe, just maybe, he told himself, Goertz wouldn't nitpick too much, since he had shown so little real interest in Lu's thesis all along.

Lu arrived for the 5 P.M. session a few minutes early, wearing his best suit and favorite tie, and a white shirt that he had starched and ironed himself the night before. But it wasn't until just as everyone was walking into the conference room that (Lu later claimed) Goertz told him he was to deliver a ten- to fifteen-minute oral précis of his thesis before the panelists would begin their questioning of him. This left Lu speechless.

He had not come prepared to give an opening talk! Who could summarize such a complicated, 10,000-word thesis with no advanced notice? And how could he do a thorough job without his slides? This latest outrage sent Lu's mind spinning; he was convinced that the treacherous Goertz had deliberately hurled yet another obstacle in his way.

In reality, it's hard to believe that any Ph.D. candidate wouldn't be keenly aware that a brief oral presentation always was expected at the start of a dissertation defense. "An oral presentation is standard. It's the normal way we do it," said Dr. Donald Gurnett, a member of Lu's committee that day. "Usually, when the student walks in, the thesis adviser will say, 'Please make a ten- to fifteen-minute oral presentation.' That's pretty much the tradition." All oral examinations are widely advertised, and are open to the

general public. If Lu truly did not know that an oral
presentation was expected of him, Gurnett said, "All I can
think of is that he somehow missed [hearing of] it."

As the onlookers settled into their chairs, Lu struggled
to regain his composure. As he walked to the chalkboard,
he told himself that—the unexpected format notwith-
standing—his work would stand on its own merits. They
might not like him as a person, but they couldn't dispute
his results. Or so he thought.

About halfway through the session, Gurnett began a
line of questioning that proved to be the turning point. Like
the other panelists, he had been provided a copy of Lu's
thesis, and had studied it thoroughly. And he had come
away impressed by it. Although Gurnett for the most part
did experimental space research, he was quite knowledgeable about the general field that Lu worked in. And Lu
knew Gurnett—he had taken a course with the professor
several years earlier, and respected him, even recommend-
ing him to others as an academic adviser.

What troubled Gurnett was that Lu had borrowed
from another student the computer program with which he
did his massive computations. "But there wasn't any
significant discussion in the thesis of how he could be sure
that the computer program had worked properly," Gurnett
recalled. "And I've had enough experience with computer
simulations to know that if you make even one little tiny
mistake—such as changing a plus sign to a minus sign—it
can completely change the results."

And so Gurnett began quizzing Lu about what sort of
quality-control tests he had run, expecting Lu to have
tested the borrowed program by running a known problem
through it with a known answer. Such an exercise would
have ensured that the program had functioned properly.

But Lu hadn't done so. And it immediately became
apparent that in fact he knew very little about the borrowed program. "I became increasingly concerned that he

didn't know there weren't mistakes when he modified the program," Gurnett recalled.

Lu, sensing the disastrous turn that the oral examination had taken, was devastated. He had absolutely no legitimate defense. "Here you had a student who didn't know the most basic things about the program at all," Gurnett said.

But soon Gurnett's time was up, and he yielded the floor to Nicholson. And the chairman immediately picked up on the same line of questioning.

A last-minute substitute for associate physics professor Robert L. Merlino, who had to leave town abruptly, Nicholson knew more than Gurnett about computer simulations, and asked Lu even more probing questions. When he inquired as to whether the borrowed computer program used a single-precision or a much more accurate double-precision procedure in doing the calculations, Lu didn't know. And this further rattled him. Now, not only did he have no answers, but also, his already-poor command of English was becoming worse by the moment. Lu was bombing out!

It was an endless and utterly humiliating experience for Lu—an increasingly uncomfortable one for Professor Goertz. As the grilling persisted, Goertz shifted more and more uneasily in his seat. He felt defensive. And for good reason: He was, after all, Lu's thesis adviser. When he could restrain himself no more, he rose expressing his confidence in the computer program and noting that he'd previously worked with several other students who also had used it. Still, he had to concede that there simply was no evidence in Lu's thesis that he had done the double-precision calculations necessary to ensure accuracy.

This shortcoming had to be immediately addressed, and the opinion of the panelists was unanimous: Double precision is a standard backup procedure to eliminate any possibility of round-off errors—a potential pitfall when working with massive numbers and equations that require exquisite precision.

"You need to go back and redo your calculations, verifying that the program was accurate," Nicholson told Lu. The candidate blinked back his shock. True, he had done his computations only once—but he was dead certain of his results. There was *no* possibility of a round-off error!

But there was also no room for argument. Until Lu did his additional computer calculations and verified the validity of his results, his dissertation would go unsigned. He also was asked to do some minor rewriting of several sections of his thesis.

Lu now blamed both Goertz and Nicholson for brutally exposing him to humiliation and causing him emotional anguish. He was as shaken as he was livid. "He took small things that are quite normal, like checking the facts in a thesis, and made them into a personal insult of great magnitude. He made them much bigger and more evil when they were actually quite innocent," said one physics department member.

After the session, which had lasted well over an hour, Goertz was sufficiently chagrined that he went up to Gurnett's office to continue the discussion, still upset over the way things had worked out. But Goertz left convinced that the right course of action had been taken. All Lu had to do was recheck his calculations, and test the program's integrity, by running through some known problems. "It was entirely appropriate that the committee caught Lu's oversight and forced him to recalculate," said Leslie B. Sims, dean of the graduate college.

As Lu stalked home that Monday evening, he could not help but recall the party he had attended just six months earlier—to celebrate Shan's passing of the oral examinations. Once more, Lu felt the sting of having been eclipsed by Shan.

He now also cursed associate professor Robert A. Smith, who was both close to Goertz, and a rising star in the department. Smith had been on the oral-examinations committee, and Lu felt that Smith also had been too critical in questioning his work. Lu further blamed Smith for having successfully persuaded Goertz and Nicholson to allow Shan to graduate ahead of some of the others, including Lu, even though Shan had missed a deadline for graduation paperwork.

After Lu's disastrous defense of his thesis, Goertz also was annoyed at Nicholson, whom he felt had been too bent on flustering Lu. "Lu Gang made a fool of himself," Goertz told his wife, Ulrike, that Monday night. Mrs. Goertz, in an interview with the *Los Angeles Times*, also quoted her husband as having said: "Lu Gang did not defend himself well, but you should not humiliate a student the way Dwight Nicholson did."

Despite his setback on April 22, Lu had no time to wallow. He needed to complete his dissertation requirements—but he also needed to find a job, or at least some source of stopgap income, fast. Because, after nearly six years under its protective wing, he had just eighteen more days left on the university's payroll. Thus he viewed with a special sense of urgency the looming entry deadline for the university's annual D. C. Spriesterbach Dissertation Prize. It carried a $2,500 cash award.

The prize, which recognizes excellence in doctoral research, is given by the University of Iowa Foundation each year. Eligibility rotates among four broad disciplinary areas: the humanities and fine arts, mathematics and the physical sciences, the biological sciences, and the social sciences. The award was created in 1981 in honor of a professor emeritus who, during a forty-one-year career at the university, taught speech pathology, and served as dean of the graduate college—and later as vice president for educational development and research. In 1991 the competition was to be in mathematics and the physical sciences, and that meant that Lu's department would be allowed to submit one nomination, to be chosen by the department chairman. And, as fate would have it, that was of course Dwight Nicholson.

To be eligible, the signed dissertation of a Ph.D. student graduating in May had to be formally accepted by the Graduate College by Monday, April 29—only a week away. So, within hours of staggering angrily out of his oral examinations, Lu was back at work. And for the rest of that week, Lu spent virtually day and night running massive computations through the mainframe computers, and re-working certain sections of his thesis.

By the early hours of Thursday morning, Lu was done. And he was exhilarated. His numbers absolutely checked out—just as he knew they would. The double-precision computations ordered by Nicholson had been a total waste of time! Within hours, he had his revised dissertation on Nicholson's desk, and the chairman signed it later that day. So did Professor Smith.

In quick succession, the other three panelists also signed Lu's 188-page thesis. "He came up to my office and discussed his revisions with me," Gurnett recalled. "His attitude was a bit reserved, but we had a pleasant conversation over the steps he had taken to satisfy my reservations. I spent quite a bit of time trying to assure him that this was all for the best—that he would want his thesis to be the best possible, since it will be bound and stored in the library forever, as testimony to his work. But I could tell he still felt it had been a blow." In fact, Lu continued to labor under the misimpression that Gurnett and Nicholson had questioned the basic scientific *principle* of his thesis.

In any case, Lu at last had overcome the panelists' every objection, and they had all signed his dissertation. It was deposited with the Graduate College in plenty of time. Though physically drained, Lu felt pure elation: He had met his deadline; he had shown them all to be wrong. Now he would graduate in May. And, most of all, his thesis would be considered by Nicholson as the department's nomination for the Spriesterbach Award.

Lu was sure that his entry would get the nod from Nicholson. He would bet his life on that.

ELEVEN

A Rush to Judgment

On Friday, April 26, Lu Gang gave himself the rare luxury of sleeping in, not stirring until almost noon. But when he did finally awaken, his mind snapped to attention: Even with twelve hours of sleep, Lu was still bone-weary from the frenetic, sleep-deprived week he'd endured while revising his thesis. Now he was operating on pure adrenaline.

Despite his mortifying experience with the dissertation committee four days earlier, Lu already was more or less over it. It was time to look ahead, and he certainly had plenty to feel good about. In fact, he was filled with a mix of self-appreciation and righteous indignation.

Hadn't he vindicated himself after doing the massive computer recalculations? His numbers were perfect the *first* time. He had manfully taken everything that Nicholson and Goertz threw at him, and he was still standing tall. And now his enemies had finally run out of ammunition and excuses. There was nothing left for them to possibly find fault with. Nicholson and Goertz, along with Bob Smith, could help Shan Linhua all they wanted, but they could no longer deny Lu Gang. The cowboy was going to prevail after all!

After so much unnecessary grief, his dissertation would at last be considered for the Spriesterbach Award. There was a two-year window of eligibility for the 1991 competition: A student must have received his or her doctorate, or at least have completed its degree requirements, between July 1, 1989, and June 30, 1991. The criteria were originality, and degree of contribution to one's field of study. The winner not only would receive a $2,500 cash prize, but also automatically become the university's nominee in the national competition for the Council of Graduate Schools' annual dissertation prize. In past years, numerous Spriesterbach Award winners ended up as finalists in the national competitions, and several years earlier, the university's David Lasocki, a music professor who had won the Spriesterbach Award, went on to capture the national title.

Lu had little to do that Friday: His academic work was behind him. Still, he quickly got dressed and walked the two short blocks along tree-lined Jefferson Street, to Van Allen Hall. Inside, as usual, Lu did not bother to wait for an elevator. He bounded up the stairs, all the way to his fifth-floor office—the one he shared with other graduate students, including Shan Linhua, whose desk adjoined his.

Lu went to the office with the intention of tidying things up and then resuming his job-hunting efforts. But first he had to clean off his desk. It was strewn with mounds of papers, textbooks, and assorted reference materials, evidence of a backbreaking week that was now, thankfully, at an end. His workspace stood in stark contrast to the uncluttered desk of his neighbor.

Shan's desk had on it just a single piece of paper. It appeared to be a letter. Upon looking closer, Lu saw from the letterhead that it was a memo to Shan from Nicholson—dated that very day.

Now that is was the lunch hour, the office was all but

deserted. Lu stopped sorting through his own papers, looked around, and picked up the tempting missive. The opening words made him gasp with disbelief.

It was a congratulatory note. Nicholson was informing Shan that he had decided to nominate Shan's dissertation as the department's candidate for the Spriesterbach Award. The memo explained the selection process, and detailed the necessary paperwork required to formalize Shan's nomination.

Now Lu was in shock. This was incomprehensible! Even as he was still revising his dissertation at Nicholson's direction, the department head already had decided, behind his back, to nominate Shan.

How grossly unfair, Lu thought, his mind in turmoil. How could anyone in good conscience have compared an unfinished dissertation, still undergoing revisions, to all the others? Why didn't Nicholson wait just a few more days—until Lu had finished revising his thesis? What was Nicholson's hurry: The deadline for submitting a physics department nominee to the Graduate College wasn't until July 12!

There could be only one explanation, Lu decided: This was just one more cowardly act of sabotage designed to block him. In a blind fury Lu stormed down to the second floor, to confront Nicholson. The chairman wasn't surprised by Lu's tirade, but rather had a ready explanation. He said that he was already extremely familiar with Lu's dissertation, having sat as a member of his oral examination committee earlier in the week. Lu's revisions, Nicholson pronounced, in no way could have improved the thesis to the point of overtaking Shan's.

Nicholson had made his decision well before the official deadline in part because he had a penchant for getting ahead of himself when it came to administrative work. This practice helped enable him to spend "quality time" with Jane on their designated weekends together. He did not, however, bother explaining this to Lu, believing it to be a personal matter that didn't concern students.

Even if Nicholson had taken the time to fully confide in Lu, it most likely would not have made any difference. Already feeling more alienated and hostile than ever toward Nicholson, Lu probably couldn't have been disabused of the notion that the chairman was in a conspiracy with Goertz and Smith to stymie his aspirations.

But Lu couldn't have been more mistaken. Nicholson was one of the best friends that any foreign student could ever have—especially one from China. He particularly admired the Chinese students for their abilities. Indeed, of the eight doctoral students whose dissertations Nicholson supervised at Iowa, four were Chinese.

But as far as Nicholson was concerned, the issue was closed. The chairman remained polite yet firm, keeping his composure even as his charge's face reddened and his body shook with barely controlled rage. Finally, Lu simply stormed out.

Lu was not one to give up so easily, however. He pursued the matter with Nicholson again on the very next day—at the department's annual spring picnic. Of all the department's social functions, this was always the best-attended. Nearly everyone showed up, bringing their spouses and children for a relaxing day of picnicking, softball, volleyball, and children's games. It was hardly the appropriate time or place for what he had in mind, but Lu seemed neither to notice nor to care.

Bitterly and shrilly he complained about his treatment, accusing Nicholson of not having given him a fair shake. Lu told him that his actions amounted to "a brutal violation" of university policy. When Nicholson tried patiently once more to set him straight, Lu angrily accused him of having abused his authority as chairman.

After a while, Lu finally realized that it was pointless

to continue. He was only making a spectacle of himself, and at the same time providing more fodder for his enemies in the department. His only recourse, he realized, was to take his case to higher authorities.

If Nicholson was troubled by Lu's accusations, he so confided in no one—not even Jane. But then, he rarely did when it came to departmental matters. In all their years, only once or twice did he invoke the name of a colleague. "Dwight was the kind of person who made things look easy. He simply had this gift," Jane recalled. "I never knew if he had disagreements with colleagues or students. But he must have."

Shortly after his unpleasant encounters with Lu, during a long-distance call in the early summer of 1991, Nicholson rather casually mentioned to Jane that a student had filed a grievance complaint against him. "But don't worry," he told her. "It's completely under control."

TWELVE

Seeking Redress

There were many Asians in Iowa City, and in particular university students—but rarely did any of them show up where Marjorie Stanton worked. Although basically the weapons clerk in the records section of the Johnson County Sheriff's Office, Stanton doubled as the department's information clerk, regularly staffing the front counter in the lobby. Thus she was the first person a visitor encountered upon entering the modern, red-brick jail house on South Capitol Street at the edge of downtown. If anyone (Asian or otherwise) wanted to obtain a permit to buy a gun, Stanton certainly was the right public servant (as well as the easiest) to see, right off the bat.

On the morning of May 21, 1991, Stanton's interest was immediately piqued when a short, somewhat slight Chinese man entered, whom she quickly sized up as a university graduate student. He looked around with uncertainty as he approached the information counter where Stanton sat. He wanted to know how to get a permit, so he could buy a gun.

On any given business day, the Sheriff's office issued at least five gun permits, and sometimes as many as twenty—but almost never to a university student. And rarer still to an Asian-American. Most unusual of all, no foreign-national had ever before sought a gun permit from the Johnson County Sheriff's Office.

But Stanton treated Lu Gang like anyone else, politely giving him information about the proper procedures and requirements. He seemed surprised by how easy it was. He could initiate the process on the spot, and have the license, and a gun, in just three days—provided, of course, that everything checked out.

Stanton handed him a one-page application form to fill out. Besides his address and date of birth, the form simply posed twelve true-or-false questions seeking information about the applicant's age (twenty-one was the minimum requirement) and whether he or she had committed any crimes. For Lu, the only possible hitch came on the final question, which asked about citizenship. But that wouldn't be a barrier either, Stanton assured him, as long as he had been in the state for at least ninety days and in Johnson County for at least thirty. No problem, Lu said with a smile, visibly relieved.

Making no effort at small talk, Lu completed the application form and handed it back to Stanton. He also had to produce his Iowa driver's license, to satisfy identification requirements. As a renter, he also was required by law to produce a copy of a recent utility bill that bore his name and current address. In this case, Lu was caught unprepared—but that also was no big deal, Stanton told him. He could bring one with him in three days—when he came to pick up his license (assuming that he had cleared the routine background check in the interim). Lu thanked her and left, saying he would return promptly.

After Lu had departed, Stanton consulted with her boss, Sheriff Robert Carpenter, about the unusual applicant. Puzzled, Carpenter had Stanton check with authorities at the Iowa Public Safety Department's weapons section in Des Moines. But officials there assured Stanton that there were no laws barring a foreigner from obtaining a gun permit, or owning a gun. As long as Lu—or any other foreign national—met the residency requirements, he could not be denied.

Stanton also checked Lu out with the FBI and various state law-enforcement agencies. Finally, she ran his name through Johnson County's own records—for any criminal violations, or even traffic complaints. Nothing turned up. Lu Gang was clean.

On Friday afternoon, May 24, Lu returned to pick up his permit. He had the required utility bill, and even showed Stanton his valid passport. "He had all the documentation that was required," she recalled. "It was that simple."

.   And so she fingerprinted Lu, and he plunked down a wrinkled $10 bill to pay the application fee. As Lu got ready to leave, Stanton issued just a few standard reminders: He must not take a gun out of the country, she told him. No problem Lu replied. And, whenever transporting a gun, he had to carry it in a box large enough so that it could not be concealed on his person. That was a state law. Lu nodded as he neatly folded his gun permit and tucked it inside his wallet.

Lastly, Stanton told him, the permit was good for only one year. Then he would have to return to renew it. Yes, yes, Lu replied, somewhat absentmindedly. But that really wouldn't be necessary.

*   *   *

Lu spent a good part of that weekend poring over the endless array of ads in *Handguns* magazine, familiarizing himself with firearms. He had no interest in the rifles.

On May 29, just five days after getting his gun permit, Lu walked into Ammo Bearer Ltd., the one store in Iowa

City that sold only firearms. Unlike most gun aficionados, Lu seemed uncertain about what he wanted, and was uneasy handling a weapon in a way that immediately marked him as a novice. Eventually he settled on a .25-caliber pistol and some bullets, charging the $101.87 on his Visa card. All he had to show was his gun permit and a photo-I.D.

Lu wasted little time trying out the weapon, visiting several shooting ranges in the area. "He was a loner," recalled Bill Sterner, a range officer at the West Liberty Gun Club. Sterner, an electrician by trade, worked as a volunteer at the range, which was open only on weekend afternoons. Trained by the National Rifle Association (NRA), his responsibility was to ensure that patrons conducted themselves in a safe manner.

The club had thirty firing stations, indoors and out, plus a trap range for shotguns. Lu stood out in Sterner's memory largely because he seemed so out-of-place. Whereas most customers arrived at the range with friends, Sterner said, "Lu Gang never came in with anyone else. And he never said a word to anybody."

Sterner would help him get set up, but then Lu would quietly put in his ear plugs and be content to be left alone with his weapon and his own thoughts. He preferred the outdoor range.

What neither Sterner nor anybody else at the gun club could have known was that, as Lu took aim at the pole-mounted, official NRA targets, he saw not the black-and-white concentric circles with a bull's-eye in the middle, but the faces of his hated nemeses:

Chris Goertz, the abusive Nazi asshole. *Pow!*
Dwight Nicholson, the vainglorious politician. *Pow!*
Bob Smith, the self-serving saboteur. *Pow!*
Shan Linhua, the ass-kissing country bumpkin. *Pow!*

After nearly two months of steady practice, including a few illegal outings at Kent Park, Lu became proficient with his weapon. At the gun clubs, his favorite firing position was from a distance of fifty feet, and under timed and rapid-fire conditions.

Soon Lu grew tired of the .25-caliber handgun; he wanted something more powerful. At the end of July, he went to Fin and Feathers, a huge sporting-goods store in town, traded in his pistol and paid $179.99 for a .38-caliber Taurus. The Brazilian-made Taurus was designed as a clone of the powerful Smith & Wesson handgun that was favored by police departments all over the country.

Lu immediately loved the feel of the Taurus. It was both sleek and compact enough to easily go unnoticed in the pocket of a jacket. Yet it packed a wallop guaranteed to stop an enemy—a human enemy—in his tracks.

But Lu also wanted to give himself a little extra margin for error. And so, a week later, on August 8, he returned to Ammo Bearer and bought a really small pistol—a .22-caliber Jennings. This he intended to use only as a backup.

*   *   *

In the final summer of his life, Lu Gang's daily existence became steeped in vicarious, anticipatory violence. When he wasn't at some pistol range he was home alone on a cheap sofa, watching action-packed, violence-filled movies rented from Budget Video. Aside from Clint Eastwood films, Lu especially enjoyed *No Way Out*, *Die Hard*, and the *Indiana Jones* series.

Lu had seen his first American movie on a January night in 1986. To celebrate passing his comprehensive examinations, thus officially qualifying for the Ph.D. program, he had rented *About Last Night*, with Demi Moore and Rob Lowe. But Lu had different tastes now. In his increasingly shrinking world, he had developed an insatiable appetite for films in which a lonely hero fought the evil establishment. The longer the odds, the better. The more violent, the better—as long as the bad guys got it in the end.

Lu had endless time on his hands now. He had gone off the university payroll as of May 11, and he passed his days by watching videos. They helped take his mind off things, providing a respite from the festering anger. He was still welcomed at the physics department, whether for a social event or the weekly informal discussions on Friday afternoons, but he rarely went anymore. And even when he did show his face at Van Allen Hall, he was stoically distant, barely bothering to exchange pleasantries with the others.

By the summer of 1991, Lu had cut himself off so completely that his family members in China became concerned. The fact was that he was so miserable that he felt he had nothing good to write home about. When Feng Wei, one of Lu's physics classmates, went home to Beijing that summer, Lu's brother-in-law brought over a suitcase brimming with herbs and other Chinese delicacies for delivery to Lu in Iowa. The in-law them bombarded Feng with questions about Lu. And Zheng Feng, a high school classmate of Lu's wrote to him from China: "Your father urged me to contact you...telling me that from Spring Festival (in January) until now, you have never written a single word to your family, and your mother was worried about you."

Recalled physics professor Gerald L. Payne, "He really distanced himself from the Chinese community. *They* may have known, but *we* certainly didn't know he was so isolated."

Payne was right. Many of Lu's compatriots were well aware that Lu believed himself as ostracized and alienated. But most of the Chinese students wisely stayed clear of him, feeling that he was to blame for his problems. "If he talked this out with someone in the final days, things might have been different," said Fan Fan, the graduate biochemistry student. "But he had no one to talk to. It became a dead-end street, and he couldn't get out. He just became too determined to carry out his plans."

Added physicist John Lyons: "You'd like to think that there could have been something done to prevent this...."

Perhaps so, for it was only gradually, after all, that Lu sank into the abyss. Yet such second-guessing ignores the fact that, like most mass murderers, Lu was essentially a loner. His vast personal collection of snapshots confirms that. Utterly alone, he traveled all over the United States, faithfully documenting his sojourns with a 34-millimeter camera.

During a winter break in 1987, just months after returning from Europe, Lu went to Colorado to see the ski resorts. In Denver, he bought a white cowboy hat and toured the nearby Rocky Mountain foothills by bus. During spring break the following year he visited the Gulf beaches in Texas, where he met up with a group of students from the East who threw raucous beach parties that included wet T-shirt contests. In Central Florida, he toured Disney World and Epcot, taking pictures of himself by remote control. In Las Vegas, he roamed the casinos, trying his luck at blackjack. In his white cowboy hat, brown leather jacket, and oversized sunglasses that bracketed his long, out-of-fashion sideburns, Lu stuck out like a sore thumb as he strolled up and down The Strip, gaping in awe at the dazzling pleasure-palace lights.

* * *

As the spring of 1991 eased into summer, Lu was still unemployed, and his agitation approached the danger point. When he wasn't target-shooting at the range, or watching movies, he sat hunched over his personal computer at home, sending out an occasional résumé—but mostly composing letters to University of Iowa officials, protesting Nicholson's nomination of Shan Linhua's dissertation for the Spriesterbach Award.

Convinced that he could no longer get a fair hearing within the physics department, Lu was now taking his case to the university's central administration. It would be his final peaceful attempt to have his grievances addressed. If this led nowhere, then all bets were off. He would have no choice but to take other and "extraordinary" measures. Lu was giving the university's top officials a chance to stop the injustice and the conspiracy against him. It was now in their power to avoid the bloodshed. But if they didn't, it all would be their fault—not his.

On June 13, barely two weeks after obtaining his first handgun, Lu wrote to James F. Jakobsen, associate dean of the Graduate College, asking for information about the Spriesterbach Award. Specifically, Lu wanted to know, who is eligible? Jakobsen telephoned Lu and told him that competition was open only to those nominated by their own academic departments.

Six days later, Shan's nomination by Nicholson was officially sent to the Graduate College. On that same day, June 19, Lu launched his formal complaint.

In a letter to Susan L. Mask, director of the office of affirmative action, Lu accused Nicholson of violating university policy on equal opportunity, and of not having given his dissertation fair consideration. Lu's letter, which contained numerous mistakes of fact as well as of grammar, conceded that his own thesis had been delayed "due to some unforeseeing convenience," although he did not elaborate thereon.

Lu also lied by saying that he did not learn until "months later" of Nicholson's decision to nominate Shan for the Spriesterbach Award. Lu had of course read Nicholson's April 26 memo to Shan that very day—as it lay open-faced on Shan's desk. Additionally, Lu accused Nicholson of uttering falsehoods: "I think he was lying by saying he considered my thesis for the nomination," Lu wrote to Mask. "I am not sure whether his such action is intentional or not. I think his action is a brutal violation of the university policy. I believe in the university community everyone deserves a fair treatment from the administration. But it seems to me that Dr. Nicholson was abusing his authority as a departmental chair in the handling of this matter which really damages the image of the university," he wrote.

"I think," he continued, "the current nomination should be nullified to preserve the reputation of the university."

In conclusion, Lu wrote: "I have spent almost six years in this university and I am very proud of having a degree conferred by this university which is famous for its academic/scientific excellences. I really hate to see such a fine university being ruined by a few executives like Dr. Nicholson who disrespect the university's policies for their own personal/political interest. I sent him a note in the morning of June 17 to ask him for a sincere explanation, he has not replied yet."

Susan Mask's office responded to Lu expeditiously. In a letter dated June 24, compliance officer Marie Prince-Martin told him that her office would investigate his claim *if* he was of the belief that Nicholson's actions "constituted discrimination on the basis of race, national origin, religion, age, gender, disability, Vietnam-era veteran status, or disabled veteran status...." But first Lu needed to file a formal complaint, and to do that required Lu to come in and "discuss the specifics" with either Prince-Martin or Mask.

On that same day, Lu received another letter also dated June 24. It was from Rudolph W. Schulz, acting dean of the Graduate College. He informed Lu, in a one-paragraph letter, that there was nothing to his complaint. After looking into the matter, Schulz said, the Graduate College found "no justification for nullifying" Nicholson's nomination of Shan. The procedures followed by Nicholson, he wrote, "seem to us to have been reasonable and to have involved a considerable amount of consultation by the chair with members of the faculty. We have been assured that your dissertation was among those considered...."

If Lu felt little encouragement after reading Prince-Martin's letter, he became livid when he read Schulz's curt reply, especially when he noticed at the bottom of the letter that Schulz had sent a copy to Nicholson. Lu saw this as the beginning of a university-wide coverup; he was convinced that officials were closing ranks. And now Nicholson was sure to retaliate, no doubt by trying to sabotage Lu's job-hunting efforts.

Within hours of receiving Schulz's letter, Lu dashed off a reply, expressing shock at Schulz's "dismissal" of his complaint. Indignantly, he demanded an independent investigation. Nothing short of that, he said, would preclude his taking "further action, whatever necessary, to protect my rights."

But Lu's letter to Schulz arrived too late. By then, Leslie B. Sims had assumed the job of dean of the Graduate College. And with summer vacations in full swing, Lu's letter didn't reach the busy new dean's desk for several weeks. When at last Sims did read the letter, he became immediately troubled by its tone. "I felt very strongly that it needed attending to in an expeditious manner," Sims recalled. "His wording—especially that phrase about 'protecting my rights'—made me think that he was very, very upset about this."

Sims called Lu immediately and invited him in for a face-to-face discussion. But Lu rejected the offer, as earlier he had rejected Prince-Martin's written invitation to talk about his grievance with the affirmative action office. "He said he didn't want to come in to talk. He preferred to have it all in writing. He wanted to have full documentation," Sims recalled.

Nevertheless, the new dean quickly set out to conduct

his own inquiry. Sims was not daunted by the fact that Lu's complaint involved the physics department, or that scientific issues were at the core of the controversy. A friendly, soft-spoken man with a quick smile and sharp eyes, Sims was a trained scientist—and a widely published research chemist. But at the age of forty-two, while a professor at the University of Arkansas in 1979, he agreed to serve as chairman of chemistry, thus embarking on a career as a university administrator. Before arriving at the University of Iowa in 1991, he had served as North Carolina State University's associate vice chancellor for research.

Being new to the university, Sims consulted widely with his colleagues as well as with staff aides at the Graduate College, asking probing questions about procedures involving the Spriesterbach Award. He also carefully examined the documents on file pertaining to Lu's complaint. Then he had a long conversation with Dwight Nicholson.

The physics chairman spoke candidly with Sims, reassuring him that he (Nicholson) had religiously adhered to all departmental procedures and guidelines in nominating Shan's dissertation. They were the same procedures and guidelines that had been in force for several other competitions, and no one had raised any questions about them. The bottom line was that Shan's thesis was superior to Lu's.

Satisfied at last, the dean sent Lu an expansive letter, on August 2, a Friday, saying that he concurred with Schulz's finding that Lu's dissertation indeed had been among the fifteen that Nicholson considered, and that Nicholson had ranked it among the top three or four. But only one could be selected, and Sims said he was convinced that Nicholson's selection of Shan's thesis had been made "on a sound, objective basis...."

Unlike Schulz, Sims went on to compliment Lu for an outstanding academic career. But in the end, he did not mince words: "There is no basis for the Graduate College to nullify the selection of the physics department for the Spriesterbach Award," Sims wrote. Sensing that the letter wouldn't satisfy Lu, however, he closed with this earnest invitation: "If you wish, I would be happy to talk with you about this matter, and I urge you to do so if you still feel you have any basis for further complaint."

What Sims did not disclose to Lu were a few other things that Nicholson had said to him about Lu. "This could be very damaging to Lu," Nicholson had told Sims, urging him to keep the case in low profile. If word of Lu's complaint circulated, the student would surely be branded a troublemaker, and some of the professors might not write helpful letters of recommendation for him, Nicholson said.

"This guy's a genius. Both are geniuses. But Shan Linhua is just more of a genius," Nicholson told Sims. "I want Lu Gang to get a good job. He's got a great future in the profession."

*   *   *

Sim's letter arrived in Lu's mailbox on Saturday, and on the next morning Lu sat down to compose a reply. It had taken him a full day to digest it and try to get over his anger enough to answer it.

"I don't think I agree with you in this matter," Lu began. "It seems to me that all your conclusions are based upon Dr. Nicholson's words because you are 'assured' no wrong doing [is] involved in this matter. However, did Dr. Nicholson tell you what he was doing in my Ph.D. defense?"

Lu then repeated his claim that he had been totally unaware that he was to have given an oral presentation at the start of his thesis defense. He wrote: "I was totally taken out of guard and consequently my performance was a little disappointing which is quite understandable."

Still struggling with his grammar, Lu went on to

contend that Nicholson "should have waited until all Ph.D. candidates actually finish their thesis or approved by their committees before he made his nomination." Lu added: "My thesis was not finished yet at the time of his nomination [of Shan]." This action Lu characterized as "analogue to" a football referee declaring a team the winner at the end of only three quarters of play.

Lu's bitterness fairly poured out: "I believe this is a public university where every person should be treated equally. In the nomination process, every Ph.D. graduate should be given a fair consideration in the beginning even only one nomination will be made at the end," he wrote. "I believe Dr. Nicholson is not fair in the nominating process by willful neglection of some potential nominees for his own, non-academic purpose, and consequently he committed a fraud. I think Dr. Nicholson should be penalized for his fraud to preserve the reputation and dignity of the university. Any attempt to cover this up by any person or organization will not help the image of the university already damaged by some previous, unfortunate situations."

Lu's calculated reference to the sexual harassment case of Dr. Jean Jew was a bluff. He had no intention of spending his hard-earned money to hire a lawyer to sue the university. Bullets were much cheaper. Still, Lu closed his letter to Sims with the ostentatiously clumsy request that "we keep mutual communications by written letters which can be kept as potential evidence."

Lu also had some unsolicited advice for the new dean. "If I were you, I would either hold a hearing where both sides can argue for themselves, supported by their evidence/witness, or at least a signed affidavit from every one mentioned in this complaint regarding this matter will certainly help a fair processing of my complaint."

Much to his credit, Sims continued giving Lu's case

top priority, responding to his August 4 letter immediately. Once more, Sims tried to explain his ratification of Rudolph Schulz's ruling that Lu's complaint was without merit. "I will try again to state the basis of that decision," Sims began his letter of August 6.

"The technical fact that your Graduate Advisory Committee required changes in your dissertation and withheld formal approval until Thursday, April 25 [when Nicholson and Smith signed the thesis] or April 29 [when the other three committee members signed it] and that the thesis was not formally acceptable until Monday, April 29, does not preclude Dr. Nicholson making a selection of the departmental nominee on April 26, after he and Dr. Smith had approved a final version on April 25," Sims wrote.

He continued: "The [criteria of] 'originality' and 'significance to the field' of your work would certainly have been evident on April 26 to anyone as familiar with your thesis as Dr. Nicholson, as a member of your committee. Further, Dr. Nicholson did not make his decision without being aware of the opinions of other faculty in the department who were at least as knowledgeable about your work as he was. Thus, while the difficult selection of one nominee from three or four strong contenders was made by Dr. Nicholson, I am completely satisfied it was consistent with all the evidence and judgments brought to bear on the decision."

For a fleeting moment, Sims allowed his irritation to show. While every candidate has a right to have his dissertation scrupulously weighed, he wrote, "no one has a right to be the selected nominee." Then Sims reiterated, as unequivocally as he knew how: "My decision is that your doctoral work was closely examined and carefully considered by the Department of Physics...."

In closing, Sims tried to get Lu to see the futility of pressing his case further:

"I congratulate you for the excellent record in the Department of Physics at the University of Iowa. I find no negative connotation in the fact that someone else was selected for the prize; on the contrary, I find it a very positive reflection that your work was so highly rated as to put yours in the top three or four among approximately 15 dissertations produced in the department during the preceding two-year period."

Sims extended his combination pat-on-the-back and wakeup call:

"I am confident you will continue to develop an excellent professional career, during which you will no doubt gain recognition, perhaps even prizes, for your work, but during which you may also at times not be the person selected from among your colleagues for certain distinctions and awards. It is the mark of a true professional to accept the judgment of one's peers and to profit by the criticism of the research community. Those who persevere and continue to produce excellent work will be rewarded with the satisfaction attendant to good scholarship and with the recognition of one's professional peers."

But Sims's final paragraph slammed the door shut:

"The Graduate College administers the D. C. Spriesterbach Award and, as Dean, I am the arbitrator of any questions concerning the administration of the award. My decision is, therefore, final, and unless some material evidence previously unknown to me is produced, I consider this matter settled."

Still, Lu pressed on. On August 10, he wrote to Peter E. Nathan, vice president for academic affairs and dean of the faculties, saying he was doing so on the advice of the university ombudsman. In the letter, Lu reiterated his complaints in considerable detail.

In a reply four days later, Nathan told Lu that he was

referring the matter to T. Anne Cleary, the associate vice president for academic affairs. She was the person with the direct responsibility for investigating such matters. "I will share a copy of your letter with her," Nathan wrote. "I suspect she will want to see you at some point in her investigation."

On August 28, the opening day of the fall semester, the Spriesterbach Award selection committee announced the winner of the 1991 prize: Shan Linhua. Lu read about it the next day in the *Daily Iowan*. There was no more doubt in his mind now that any university official connected with the case, even those freshly drawn into the controversy, would be automatically biased against him. They were all therefore to be considered evil—and that included Anne Cleary.

Ironically, Cleary's affection for China and the Chinese was probably unrivaled in all of Iowa. She had been born in Shanghai fifty-six years earlier. Her father was a foreign-service officer in China during the 1930s, and later represented a Western cosmetics firm there. Having grown up in a French concession, she had developed a lifelong fascination with—if not to say a love for—China.

*   *   *

For a month, Lu heard nothing from Cleary. And his patience was running out. On September 6, he wrote her a letter. She called him five days later. Lu came away from their thirty-five-minute telephone conversation with the impression that his complaint had little credibility with Cleary. "I will have to call you back," Cleary told him at the end of the call.

Two days later, on September 13, Lu made what he considered his "final good faith attempt" to resolve the matter within the university setting. He wrote Hunter R. Rawlings III, president of the university, alleging that the Graduate College had now joined the physics department in a "cover up" of Nicholson's misconduct. Alluding once more to the sexual harassment case of Jean Jew, which had cost the university over $1 million, Lu urged Rawlings to conduct a fair and expeditious investigation.

Hardly confident that Rawlings would take his advice, however, Lu also proceeded down another avenue. He decided to take his appeal to the court of public opinion. Even the news media in China, after all, were now practicing a modicum of investigative journalism. Surely reporters in America would gladly look into this case of injustice and malfeasance. And the resulting publicity would most certainly force the university to act.

On September 17, Lu composed what amounted to a press release, and sent copies to the *New York Times*, the *Los Angeles Times*, the *Chicago Tribune*, the *Des Moines Register*, and KGAN-TV in Iowa City. Once more he laid out his case, concluding: "Outraged by the downright attempt to cover up, Mr. Lu is more determined to pursue a fair resolution to this matter at any cost. And he is considering to take possible legal action if he is left without other choice."

Lu mailed the letters on Wednesday, September 18, just before leaving town on a Greyhound bus for a final tour of Florida, and especially of one of his favorite haunts there—Disney World. He had last visited the theme park over the Christmas holidays in 1987, and this time found it just as engrossingly entertaining. Before leaving Orlando, he also took his fill of Sea World, another attraction that lures people back repeatedly. Then he headed for Key West, where he retraced the fabled steps of the legendary Ernest Hemingway. Lu's final stop was New Orleans, where he remembered to buy some inexpensive souvenirs at the Aquarium's gift shop before hopping on the bus for the long ride home.

*   *   *

Back in Iowa City, Lu found no relief. His press statements had drawn no discernible response. And there was no reply from Hunter Rawlings. No letter or telephone call from Anne Cleary. Nothing but silence from the university's top administrators.

As Lu dejectedly sorted through some utility bills and a bunch of junk mail, he perked up when he came across an envelope from the Center for Space Physics at Rice University in Houston, Texas. He had applied for a job there as a postdoctoral "distinguished faculty fellow," and both Goertz and Nicholson had written fine letters of recommendation on his behalf.

But even such support in that attempt had proved to no avail, as Lu could quickly see. Regretfully, Patricia H. Reiff informed him that the Center for Space Physics had been forced to reduce the pay and scope of the advertised job. "Unfortunately, one of the sources of support which we were anticipating did not materialize," Reiff wrote in her September 24 letter. "Would you still be interested if the initial term of appointment were only six months?" Lu was not.

Lu's job-hunting effort was producing nothing but an unrelenting torrent of bad news. Everywhere, money was tight and things seemed only to get worse. Even some of the top physics professors at the University of Iowa were feeling the pinch—among them Goertz, who also was running low on research funds and had openly fretted about not having some major grants renewed.

Since spring, Lu had written to nearly a hundred universities, inquiring about job possibilities. But nothing had panned out. In Fairbanks, University of Alaska officials were polite but noncommittal, promising to notify Lu "as soon as possible once we have made a final selection." In Los Angeles, California State University officials wrote: "We have received more than 500 applications for the two positions we had available. We are sorry to inform you that you were not one of the people selected." At Berkeley, Lu finished in the top ten among job applicants for an opening at the University of California's space science laboratory. Close, but not close enough. And so it went.

"There were just very few university research jobs," recalled Iowa physics professor Gerald L. Payne. "In recent years, there's been a sharp increase in the number of Ph.D. physicists, but not a corresponding increase in funding support. So you heard a lot of recent graduates complaining that they had not been warned about the over-production of Ph.Ds."

But nobody was more bitter than Lu Gang. And, with red-hot anger, he blamed on Goertz and Nicholson his inability to land a job. He was sure that Goertz, especially, was trying to keep him under his thumb, working away like a slave. That was why Goertz often missed the deadline for letters of recommendation, Lu thought. "That's the major reason that I am still jobless," he shouted at Goertz one autumn afternoon in the professor's office. Their argument was so heated that it could be heard in the hallway.

Lu became so distraught over his predicament that one September afternoon he paid another visit to Maggie Brooke in the university's office of International Education and Services. He had last visited her in May, shortly after getting his Ph.D., to obtain a pro forma "letter of practical training," a required immigration procedure that allowed a foreign student to look for a job in his field in the host country. That encounter had been rather ordinary. "I remember being happy for him that he had persisted in physics and got his degree," Brooke recalled.

But now, as he sat slumped in her office, Lu seemed a different person altogether. He was morose, and quite upset.

"I can't find a job in physics," Lu fumed, clearly feeling sorry for himself.

"Why don't you go talk to Dr. Nicholson?" Brooke suggested. "I'm sure he can help you."

Lu told her that Nicholson could not help.

Exasperated, Brooke blurted out: "Are you waiting for the American government to give you a job—like in your country? That doesn't happen here!"

What Lu wanted, it turned out, was special permission to look for a job outside his field. At the same time, he wanted to apply to the Immigration and Naturalization Service for a so-called deferred enforced departure. He didn't want to go back to China, and now there was a way to prolong his stay in the United States.

After the Tiananmen Square massacre in June 1989, President Bush had issued an executive order allowing Chinese students in the United States to delay their return until 1994. Many of them had participated in the demonstrations against the slaughter of pro-democracy forces in Beijing's central square. And Lu had been among them, joining a small group of protesters at a campus rally that paraded up and down the sidewalk. The white cardboard placard that Lu held up read "Free of Speech."

The "deferred enforced departure" order also would allow Lu to work in any job he could find. But Brooke explained to him that he might have to go to the Immigration and Naturalization Service's regional office in Omaha, Nebraska, to engineer the change in his immigration status.

At that, Lu began to whine anew. "He refused to buy what I was telling him. He said his car wasn't working. He was just very disgruntled," Brooke recalled. Nevertheless, she kept trying to cheer him up, especially praising him for having stuck it out in physics after his unsuccessful attempts, years earlier, to change his major to business administration. "I tried to get him to smile, and called him Dr. Lu," Brooke recalled.

At that, she said, Lu waved his hand dismissively.

"Don't call me that!" he shouted, his face red and contorted in anger. "It's worthless. If I can't find a job, it's not worth anything at all!" Brooke was taken aback by Lu's eruption. "I didn't know what to do. He obviously was not going to go to Omaha."

Lu left empty-handed that day. But Brooke herself followed up with the INS, and by the end of September obtained for Lu a letter allowing him to work in a field outside of physics. "He came back in and I gave him the letter, and he left. He wasn't particularly grateful," Brooke said.

Also near the end of September, Lu finally heard from Hunter Rawlings, the university's president. But his letter simply advised Lu that matters such as his complaint are normally handled by Peter Nathan, the vice president for academic affairs. "I have referred your letter to that office, and you should expect to hear from them in the near future," Rawlings wrote.

On that same day, September 27, Lu also heard at last from Anne Cleary, the busy associate vice president. She stated that she knew he wanted to file a complaint of unethical behavior against a faculty member, and enclosed a statement of professional ethics and academic responsibilities, as well as a copy of the ethics grievance procedure. Cleary also asked Lu to submit a detailed, written statement laying out his complaint, with dates and names of everyone involved. This Lu did on October 2, citing in his letter Nicholson's alleged violations of the ethics guidelines. Lu also demanded that Nicholson submit his own statement, which then should be available to Lu.

When Cleary heard from Lu, she promptly answered, confirming in an October 7 letter that Peter Nathan indeed had designated her to "promptly" make "a brief" investigation of the matter and then report back to him. "When he reaches a conclusion as to whether there is a reasonable basis for believing that the alleged misconduct has occurred, we will inform you," Cleary wrote.

But it was too late. Lu saw the handwriting on the wall, and it was all too clear. He therefore set out to bring matters to an end on his own terms. On October 8, he withdrew $10,000 from the University of Iowa Community Credit Union, and converted it into a money order at the First National Bank. Then he mailed it to Lu Huimin, his second-oldest sister—the one he had always been closest to.

Lu also had another financial transaction to complete. Unexpectedly, he had gotten a letter from Dwight Nicholson. Although addressed to him personally, it clearly was part of a mass mailing. It was a letter of solicitation, and it began with the salutation that Lu had come to despise— "Dear Dr. Lu:"

"First the good news—we're as busy as ever," Nicholson wrote. Federal funding for the physics department was at an annual record rate: $12 million. But with Iowa in a deep recession, state funding was down sharply, and *that* was why, Nicholson said, "private contributions are so important." Such funds, he explained, could help hire teaching assistants, recruit talented graduate students, and bring speakers from around the country to the department.

In better times, the department almost certainly would have found a job—perhaps a teaching assistantship, if only a part-time one—for a postdoctoral student unable to find a position elsewhere. But things were different now, and in this the department could accommodate only one postdoctoral fellowship. And that had gone to Shan Linhua.

Nicholson's solicitation letter came with a gift form and a prepaid envelope. "Of course, gifts of any size are greatly appreciated," the plea concluded. Lu pulled out his checkbook and sent in his contribution: one cent.

By the middle of October, as the university was gearing up for Homecoming Weekend, Cleary had a long talk with Les Sims about Lu's complaint. They agreed that the matter seemed unlikely to be resolved informally, and thus seemed headed for the Faculty Judicial Commission. They informed Nicholson of their conclusion, and then all three decided that it was time to apprise Goertz of Lu's complaint.

In fact, however, Goertz was already aware of the situation: Lu's complaint was widely talked about in the corridors and the lunchroom alike of Van Allen Hall—especially among the graduate students. Indeed, Goertz himself had already confronted Lu about it. During their meeting, in Goertz's office, both men were so angry and intense that neither had noticed him when James Van Allen nearly walked in on them before quickly retreating. That exchange ended with Goertz telling Lu that he was doing himself no favors by pressing his ridiculous claims.

"If you continue, it will backfire," Goertz warned, echoing Nicholson's belief that Lu could end up being branded a troublemaker, and encounter even greater difficulties in finding a job. Lu interpreted Goertz's warning altogether differently. He assumed that Goertz was trying to hush him up—part of a well-coordinated, sinister attempt by the university establishment to cover up for Nicholson.

Such treachery reminded Lu of père Alexandre Dumas's classic *The Count of Monte Cristo*, the nineteenth-century historical romance filled with intrigue, elaborate deception, and—finally—bloody revenge. Lu identified passionately with the hero, Edmond Dantès, a young sailor who is betrayed by his cohorts and ends up in prison for fourteen years while his beloved is stolen by an archenemy. Dantès eventually returns disguised as the dashing and wealthy Count, exacting swift and terrible revenge.

After his encounter with Goertz, Lu knew with absolute certainty that the only way he could prevail was to follow the example of Edmond Dantès. "Since then," Lu later wrote, "I have sworn to myself that I would revenge at any cost, soon or later."

THIRTEEN

Bitter Words

The observance of Halloween, the eve of All Saints' Day, is believed to have originated with the ancient Druids in Britain, Ireland, and France. The soothsayers, priests, judges, and poets—members and devotees of a Celtic religious order—believed that on the evening of October 31, Saman, the lord of the dead, calls forth hosts of evil spirits. Hence the Druids lit bonfires on Halloween, to ward them off.

Dwight Nicholson loved Halloween. Every year, well in advance, he stocked up on candy bars—the more the better. He could hardly wait for the evening to arrive, bringing with it the gaggles of children in every imaginable costume.

As usual, Nicholson was home alone. Normally he and Jane (who lived and worked in Tulsa) talked at 11 P.M. But this night they had their chat early: He had a bad cold, and needed rest. On the following Tuesday, he'd have to be in Tampa for a meeting of the American Physical Society's plasma division.

In Oklahoma, Jane Nicholson also was feeling a bit run-down, and looked forward to turning in early as well.

By 8 P.M., Dwight told her with a mix of great enthusiasm and relief that more than twenty kids already had come by. "He was really excited," she recalled.

*   *   *

Halloween is also regarded by some as a propitious time to reexamine one's life and contemplate the future. But for Lu Gang there was little left to consider: His future had been foreclosed. Only a few more hours remained. Eight days shy of his twenty eighth-birthday, Lu spent that night tying up the loose ends of his miserable life.

Three days earlier, Lu had withdrawn another $10,000 from the university's Community Credit Union and converted the funds into a money order at the First National Bank. Lu mailed the money order (like the earlier one for the same amount) to Huimin, his favorite sister. And that *still* wasn't all the money Lu had. Closing out all his accounts, he converted the rest of his funds into a $520 money order and a $4,793.01 cashier's check.

When Lu's first $10,000 money order arrived, Huimin was stunned. In China, that was no small fortune—and, a few weeks later, she called him from Beijing. In China it was already November 1. In Iowa City, it still was Halloween night.

Everyone in Lu's family was concerned about him. He had virtually stopped writing home, and since leaving China in 1985—more than six years earlier—he had not been back. Lu had cancelled a summer visit in 1987, in order to go to France with Goertz. And in 1989, he'd cancelled again after the Tiananmen Square incident.

Reaching her brother at home, Huimin was eager to get a sense of how he was faring.

"The security in the United States is not very good," Lu Gang told her, cryptically.

"Do you feel well?" she asked, puzzled.

"I'm okay. But I've been honest and frank for my whole

life, and I've suffered for being that sort of person," he replied. "People take advantage of me, and I feel very bad about it."

Then he changed the subject and began asking about their parents and about her child.

"He never let me know a trace of what he was about to do," Huimin later told the *Los Angeles Times*, one of the newspapers her brother had tried to interest in his case.

After the phone conversation, Lu sorted through his meager belongings. As he was doing so, he could no longer control the overwhelming sense of despair and loneliness that he felt, and soon he was overcome by a surge of emotions. Bitter over all the frustrations and rejections in a life that he no longer could control, he rued the hopelessness of it all. Lu sobbed.

When he had no more tears to shed, Lu regained his composure and continued dismantling his apartment. He disconnected his stereo system, the VCR, his telephone-answering machine, and a clock radio, loading them all into his car—the 1985 Chrysler Laser with the bumper sticker that read "I'd Rather Party at the Sports Column."

When he was finished, Lu sat down and began one final letter home—writing in neat, Chinese block characters. Addressed to "Second Elder Sister" (Huimin), Lu's letter was later translated by W. South Coblin, a professor of Chinese at the University of Iowa. The letter, in its entirety, read as follows.

> How are you! Please deposit the enclosed check in the bank speedily. This letter is written especially to you, so don't let other people in the family see it. When you read this letter, I will probably no longer be in the world of the living. I have already mailed some things back, which can be considered to constitute my legacy. I think that as long as you explain it to the customs officials, they will let these

things pass through, just as if I had brought them back myself.

What I am most worried about is our parents; they are old, and I am afraid they will not be able to bear this turmoil. But I am at the end of my resources, so this heavy responsibility must fall on your shoulders. I beg you to take care of them and spare no expenses in the effort. Moreover, don't spend any money on a funeral for me. And by all means don't come to the U.S. to take my body home. The best thing would be to let the Chinese embassy have my body cremated here in the U.S., and just send some ashes back. Keep firmly in mind that you should not let anyone here in the U.S. blackmail you into paying anything. I think the money I have sent back will suffice to repay our parents' loving kindness in raising me and the gentle care my two elder sisters gave me when I was young.

Last night when I finished talking with you on the telephone, I wept my heart out here alone. For the life of me, I can't swallow all this. You know that all my life I have been honest and straightforward, and I have most of all detested cunning, fawning sycophants and dishonest bureaucrats who think they are always right in everything. I had this in mind for a long time, but I persevered until I had taken my doctoral degree. This was an honor for the whole family. You yourself should not be too sad about it, for at least I have found a few traveling companions to accompany me to the grave.

My experiences during my 28 years have caused me to adopt a rather jaundiced view of human existence; I have on occasion said to people that I would like to take orders as a Buddhist monk. There is no end to the hopes and desires in human life. In the U.S., even though there are no worries about food and clothing, up above there are still exalted, rich people, and compared with them I am poor as a church mouse. To sum up, on my own behalf I have vented my rage, and on behalf of my family I have provided a safeguard for their livelihood.

What further expectations do I have to live for? Hence it has been said of old: "After a long drought to encounter the sweet rains, in a different place to meet an old friend, to burn the candle in one's wedding chamber, and to see one's name listed on the golden placard of successful examination candidates." I have tasted all of these four great objects of a man's life, and it can truly be said that I have known satisfaction!

Though I am single, I have had a few girlfriends. When I lived in the dormitory in high school I had already started to have girlfriends. When I went to college I often slipped into our old home at the Number 262 Hospital under cover of darkness and spent the night with girls. After I came to the States I had liaisons with Chinese and American women, with single and married women, with girls of good families and girls of the streets. I just don't have a constant heart in these matters; the grass always looks greener somewhere else, and I can't be satisfied with any particular person. Maybe I didn't meet the right one, or perhaps I thought either that they were too good for me or I was too good for them. No matter what the answer is, I feel a bit fed up with male-female relationships.

Moving on to another point, I have already lost interest in physics, at which I labored for ten years (four in college and six years in graduate school); one could say I felt more and more that I had entered a dead-end street. The study of physics is

more and more disappointing. The way it is now,
one person says one thing, another says something
else, and nobody really knows what's going on. So
people form a number of factions based around
different universities, each side attacking the other
while grandly touting their own views as correct. No
wonder that there are people who say, "Modern
physics is self-delusion." I regret a bit that at the
outset I did not study a more practical subject. But
what can be done about it now? Our parents
themselves were ignorant of these things and could
not guide me in educational matters. I had to
blunder on all by myself. Lots of Chinese physicists
with U.S. citizenship, who had been messing around
in the U.S. and weren't happy any more, returned to
China for visits and bragged that in doing so they
were making a contribution to their fatherland. And
so then the Chinese government started
propagandizing on a grand scale and beguiled the
young people into studying the theoretical sciences.

But, to get back to what I was saying earlier, if I
had at the outset studied medicine, I could not
possibly have come to the U.S. to study for a degree
and earn American currency. Our parents did not
have the economic resources to send me to the U.S.
for advanced study. Some people at this school who
are in the applied sciences, their parents are for the
most part high-level intellectuals who have studied
abroad. Their families have foreign currency, which
they can use to enable their children to take the
TOEFL and the GREs, and to defray their tuition
and living expenses. Or they have relatives living
abroad who can lend them money. That today I have
come to this pass can justly be said to be partly the
fault of our parents. I truly believe the saying, "In
life be a paragon among men, and in death be a hero

among the shades." I take personal responsibility for all that I have done.

And another thing, in the end it would be best not to let the younger generation (of our family) know how it really was with me, for it might be disadvantageous to their futures. My beloved elder sister, I take my eternal leave of you. Your younger brother.

❊   ❊   ❊

Next, Lu composed a final, public diatribe. He labeled it simply "STATEMENT"—and just under that he typed: "by Mr. Lu Gang, Ph.D." This letter he wrote in English, intending for it to get the broadest possible circulation. Law-enforcement officials released it only after deleting various vitriolic passages and specific references to various individuals. Lu's letter, transcribed here complete with grammatical mistakes and misspellings, said:

> My this life is surprisingly full of political incidents. When I was in the kindergarten, I was punished by the baby sitter for calling Mr. Lenin, the grand dad of Soviet Communism, "Bold Donkey" which is a popular insulting slung for bold people. In the last year of my junior high I was assigned to visit the memorial tomb of Chairman Mao. I showed some reluctance to the class supervisor because it was right the time for final exams. Then my public duties (vice head of the class, representative for English, Physics) were deprived. I was forced to make a self-criticism speech in front of the whole class, and all my school friends left me in the fear of political suppression. I hate politics, but I will certainly go ahead to use politics if it is my only choice to defend myself.
>
> My favorite public place in Iowa City is the

"Sports Column" where I have been around for
about five years. I made lots of good friends and
inevitably some jealous enemies there. They have
the prettiest girls in town there, and some of them
could never been forgotten such as...and the little
blonde cutie who always stays by her side. Of course
there are some girls I run into in other places, such
as...who is the sweetest girl I've ever met in this
life.

My first movie seen in the US is "About Last
Night" the evening I passed my comprehensive
exams. My favorite movies include "No Way Out,"
"Die Hard," "Indiana Jones," and Clint Eastwood's
movies where a single cowboy fights against a group
of incorporated bad guys who pick on little guys at
their will or cover up each other's ass. I believe in
the rights of people to own firearms. Historically,
gun-rights make it possible for the spread of civil
rights into the south. In those times, groups of civil
rights workers from the north were assassinated/
murdered by pro-slavery southerners, meanwhile
the local/federal authorities were reluctant to do
anything about it. So the civil rights workers have to
be heavily armed before they ever dare to enter the
south. Even today, privately-owned guns are the only
practical way for individuals/minority to protect
them against the oppression from the evil
organizations/majority who actually control the
government and legal system. Private guns make
every person equal, no matter what/who he /she is.
They also make it possible for a individual to fight
against a conspired/incorporated organization such
as Mafia or Dirty University officials. Usually an
ordinary individual is too weak, both politically and
financially, to oppose a giant organization. Fortunate
examples like Dr. Jean Dew winning a federal case

against the University of Iowa for sexual discrimination is really rare. Her success is mainly because she has a solid income (salary for a M.D. could not be bad at all) to support her five year court battle against the university of Iowa which simply neglected her complaint in the first place and issued only a public apology to her after the court's ruling in her favor. The University of Iowa even paid the fine of the primary criminal in the case (a fellow male anatomy professor), which is really outrageous. This actually indicates that this university is encouraging the male anatomy professor for his illegal behavior. It is believed that there exists no justice for little people in this world, extraordinary action has to be taken to preserve this world as a better place to live.

Christoph K. Goertz....He told me one day "you are in charge of the code and no one else knows the code"...since we are the only group to own the 2-D code right now. But as a honest human being and based upon the findings in the execution of the code, I arrived at some conclusions different from his original expectation. As a result, he became so mad that he refused to let me graduate in time for a precious job opportunity and is withholding my thesis result from being published in JGR where he serves as the chief-editor. When he couldn't find any more excuses to prevent me from graduation, he failed intentionally to notify me as it should be that I am supposed by tradition to give a 10-15 minutes talk on my thesis defense before the committee members ask me questions. In fact he told me of it until one minute before my defense started. I was taken by surprise and I had to make up a talk instantly and presented it on blackboard instead of on transparency projector. As the result, my thesis

was not passed by the committee after my defense
and I was exposed brutally to both personal
humiliation and emotional anguish....Goertz...
blamed me personally for the failure of my
defense....I did not ask him to write letters of
recommendation for job opportunities. Later when
he heard of this from Dr. Nicholson, he came to me
immediately and insist that he write such letters for
me. Goertz...missed the deadlines for most of the
letters which I had specifically specified. That is the
major reason that I am still jobless today. Then he
promised in May that he would support my work
here, however, I haven't seen any paycheck since
then while I have been working here for months
after my graduation in May. Later I made some
recent progress in extension of my thesis research
and submit it to GRL. The response from the
referees is favorably for publication after some
minor modifications. Goertz first tried to persuade
me to present it to JGR by saying that it is too
lengthy to be published in GRL. When I pointed out
that it is within the limit for GRL, he then tried to
force me to add more material to it so it will be
delayed for publication after his opinion is published
or it be forced to be submitted to JGR under his
control....

Robert Smith....Since he is new in the
department, he is eager to build his own
territory....He heard that Shan Linhua is a good
student, he then convinced Goertz to have him
graduated sooner than most of the others which of
course caused wide-spread outrage among the rest of
the students. Shan, however, missed the deadline for
graduation paperwork, then Smith went to Dwight
R. Nicholson, Chairman of the department for
personal favor which enables Shan to graduate

despite the missing of the graduate college deadline. Trying to justify his act, Smith criticizes me with his eyes closed from the facts that my way of studying the cross-field charge-separation electric field is completely wrong. At that time, everyone in the group was criticizing my study for a whole semester until I am eventually proven correct.

Dwight R. Nicholson...gave his student...an extinguished graduate fellowship even he is not qualified according the graduate college requirement. Nicholson also gave...an engineering undergraduate without even a Bachelor degree a $1/2$ time graduate research assistantship in physics. What a outrage! He committed fraud (unethical conduct) in the departmental nomination to the "D.C. Spriesterbach Dissertation Award" offered by the graduate college here which was filed by me in a series of complaints to Dr. Rudolph Schultz, Acting Dean of the Graduate College; Dr. Leslie Sims, Dean of the Graduate College; Peter Nathan, Vice President for Academic Affairs; Dr. Anne Cleary, Associated Vice President for Academic Affairs; Dr. Hunter Rawlings III, President since June 1991. The response from various university officials is, however, disappointed. Up to now, my complaints are still under primary investigation by university officials. I believe they are just trying to coordinates their words to cover this up. Immediately after Dr. Dwight Nicholson nominated Dr. Goertz for some kind of teach/research award from the university and Dr. Cleary called Dr. Goertz, Dr. Goertz came to me saying "if you continue, it will backfire." What a down-right attempt to cover-up. The whole scene looks pretty like the famous story of "The Count of Monte Cristo" by Alex Dumas. Since then I have sworn to myself that I would revenge at any cost, soon or later.

The misconducts of the said persons would be impossible without the indulgence/coverup by the university authorities. I have been revealing their unethical conducts to Dr. Rudolph Schultz, associate dean of Graduate College; Dr. Leslie Sims, dean of graduate college; Dr. Peter Nathan, Vice President for Academic Affairs; Dr. Ann Cleary, Associate Vice President for Academic Affairs; Dr. Hunter Rawlings III, President of the University of Iowa since June 1991. However, they would rather to believe the words of Nicholson than to listen to my words and my evidence. The department/college/university authorities have been in a conspiracy to isolate me, delay my complaint so I might be forced to leave here and they could claim the case dismissed because the absence of the plaintiff. I regret that I have to take extraordinary measure to resolve this matter, but it is simply not my fault. The University of Iowa authorities should be blamed for the unfortunate outcome. If the university had taken positive steps as it is supposed by the tax-payers, tuition-payers and funding agencies, all this could be avoided. The University of Iowa is trying its best to cover...Nicholson in the DCS dissertation award, in spite of the fact that I am putting my whole career on the line.

I am being a physicist who believes in the conservation of matter, energy, momentum, etc. Although my flesh/blood-made body seems dead, my spiritual soul remains perpetual and I am being quantum leaping to another corner of our world. I have finished what I am supposed to do here which is to make right what was once wrong. I am proud of my achievement here and I am more confident in my upcoming journey. So long my friends, maybe we will meet again in another time at another place. May the lord bless all those descent human beings who are honest, hard working and truthy.

*   *   *

Soon the night gave way to a reluctant dawn, densely overcast and unpromising. The day's high temperature of 57 degrees was reached in the morning, and by lunchtime the mercury was in a free-fall. A major winter storm, the first of the year, was bearing down on Iowa from the northwest.

Lu was physically exhausted and emotionally drained, but he had just a few more chores to complete. For his last meal, he walked the few short blocks to the Hamburg Inn #2, a popular diner just north of Van Allen Hall where a breakfast of three eggs and toast could be had for $1.60.

Back in his apartment on East Jefferson Street, Lu loaded his two handguns, putting one in each pocket of his brown leather jacket. Then he tucked his neatly typed public statement in his briefcase and walked the few blocks to Pak Mail, where he mailed the letter to his sister, along with the checks.

The snow flurries had turned to wet rain and sleet by the time Lu emerged from Pak Mail on Burlington Street. He looked at his watch. It was 3:20 in the afternoon. The weekly Friday seminar in Van Allen Hall was about to convene. Toting his briefcase in his left hand, Lu shoved his right hand into his coat pocket, feeling the steely power of the .38-caliber Taurus. He began striding purposefully toward Van Allen Hall.

*   *   *

Almost every year since the mid-1960s, rumors had made the rounds on college campuses that a Halloween massacre would occur at some university. Some years, the rumors were especially strong. Other years, less so.

In 1991, starting in early October, the rumor began spreading from colleges on the East Coast. Some thought a psychic who had appeared on one of the daytime television talk shows was responsible. But that could not be substantiated. In any case, no one took such talk seriously. And as soon as Halloween passed, the rumors were forgotten—put away for another year.

FOURTEEN

Physics of Revenge

One by one, they began gravitating toward room 309 in Van Allen Hall—at the end of the lengthy corridor and near both an elevator and a stairwell. There were enough chairs around the long, rectangular table and along three walls in that conference room to easily accommodate forty or more people. In this windowless setting, many of the department's plasma physics professors, researchers, and graduate students met informally on Friday afternoons to discuss their work, exchange ideas, test hypotheses, and probe one another's line of investigation. There was no telling how long these sessions would last. Sometimes they adjourned after thirty minutes; sometimes they went on for three hours or more.

Earlier that afternoon, since no one was using the room, Ji Bing, a graduate teaching assistant, had taken his work there and begun grading papers. At 3:30, he looked up to see a shuffling Lu Gang at the door, his hair soaking wet from the snow and sleet. Ji thought Lu looked tense—even grim. "Why are you here?" the puzzled Lu almost demanded of Ji, who also was from China but was not a regular member of the Friday group. Ji quickly explained. Lu reminded him of the weekly plasma session, and the two began to exchange pleasantries as Ji gathered up his papers.

On his way out, Ji saw Shan Linhua in the corridor, just beyond the doorway. They greeted one another, but Shan didn't go inside right away.

Soon the others began arriving, milling about either inside the brightly lit conference room or nearby in the hallway: Chris Goertz, Bob Smith, Paul J. Hansen, Ken Nishikawa, Robert D. Holdaway, Lyle B. Talbert, Iver H. Cairns, Nicola Dangelo, and Ebraahim Moghaddam-Taaheri.

As Lu entered, he passed Moghaddam-Taaheri, an assistant research scientist from Iran who was just finishing a last-minute cigarette in the corridor. As they walked into the conference room together, Lu absentmindedly asked him about his work.

Goertz took his customary spot at the head of the table. To his immediate left sat Nishikawa; to his right sat Smith. Most of the others took places along the side of the conference table that allowed them to easily face the chalkboard. But not Lu. He took a seat by himself, against the wall, almost directly behind Goertz.

Shan came in late. The session was already underway, and Ken Nishikawa was talking at the chalkboard. Seeing an empty chair to Goertz's immediate left (the seat vacated by Nishikawa), Shan slid into it after walking behind Goertz's back and cutting across Lu's line of vision.

Nishikawa was about ten minutes into his talk when Lu suddenly stood up and quietly exited the room. "Everybody noticed," recalled Paul Hansen.

Although his back was to Lu and the door, Goertz also saw him leave. Goertz frowned, but said nothing. It was unusual for someone to walk out like that, especially such a short time into the session. Even more unusual (although nobody really noticed it until later), Lu still had on his wet winter jacket. He obviously intended to return, though, having left his briefcase next to the chair.

Once outside room 309, Lu turned right and went down the stairwell, quickly walking down the twenty steps to the second floor. The chairman's door, as usual, was wide open. Dwight Nicholson was at his desk doing paperwork, a cup of coffee and a candy bar within reach.

His pulse racing, Lu hustled back to the third-floor conference room. He had been gone for less than a minute. Nishikawa was still talking. All was well.

Lu returned to his seat, his right hand still tucked in his coat pocket. He sat there for perhaps another minute, taking several slow, deep breaths. There was no turning back now: The time had come for sweet revenge; justice was about to be carried out.

Without so much as a word, Lu stood up—an odd, slightly lopsided smile on his face, and the cold look of fury in his eyes. As he took two steps forward, Lu in the same motion brought out the .38-caliber Taurus. He aimed it at the back of Goertz's head and squeezed the trigger. Goertz jerked and then slumped forward in his chair.

Momentarily stunned, no one in the room reacted. No one could believe what they had seen. Did a cold-blooded execution just take place before their eyes—in the middle of a colloquium on plasma physics? It didn't make sense!

Paul Hansen thought Lu was pulling some realistic-looking but silly practical joke. He silently wondered, with annoyance, "What are you doing, Lu Gang? Halloween's over." But there was nothing funny about it. Nothing at all.

A split-second later, before Goertz's body had even stopped jerking, Lu took two short steps to his left, his arm still extended. He leveled his now-smoking Taurus at Shan, the barrel of the gun just inches from Shan's forehead. Before Shan could react, Lu pulled the trigger. Shan pitched forward in his chair, the impact of the bullet knocking off his glasses.

Pandemonium erupted. People began diving under the conference table for cover. A few, near the door, made a run for it. But Bob Smith had time for neither move. Directly across the table from Shan, Smith knew he was next. "What are you doing?" Smith shouted nervously at Lu.

Lu had a cold, menacing look in eyes—but said nothing. Pointing his gun at Smith, he began advancing toward the professor, coming around the end of the conference table. ("Lu seemed quite calm and deliberate," Hansen recalled.) Trembling, Smith jumped up from his chair. But Lu was quicker. He was now between Smith and the door, blocking the only escape route. Smith began backing away, his arms half raised and half extended in a defensive posture. His voice deserted him—he simply groaned, mumbling some words that no one could understand or remember.

Lu pumped two bullets into Smith, striking him in the right hand and arm, and chest. As Smith collapsed, Lu quickly wheeled around and loped out of the room. Almost right behind him, the others scrambled madly out of the room, dashing up and down the empty corridor, yelling for help.

Lyle Talbert started running down the stairwell, heading toward the physics department's office on the second floor. But halfway down, he saw Lu not very far ahead of him, going in the same direction. Talbert abruptly backtracked. On his way back up to the third floor, he noticed some shell casings on the steps. Lu had reloaded.

Talbert ducked into room 306 for cover. Obviously the killings were not over.

Hansen and Iver Cairns were the last to crawl out from under the massive table in the conference room. They were aghast: The blood-splotched room reeked of gunpowder and death.

There was nothing they could do for Goertz or Shan. Each had a bullet hole in his skull. But Smith was still alive, bleeding profusely and gasping for breath. Cairns cradled Smith's head and gently positioned him on his back on the floor. "I can't feel anything," Smith moaned.

Hansen stuck his head out of the door and yelled for someone to call an ambulance. Just then, several more shots rang out from the floor below.

When he heard someone step into his office, Dwight Nicholson started to turn toward the door. But he never knew what hit him: Lu had come up from behind. As Nicholson turned to face him, Lu extended his Taurus toward the professor's forehead and fired. Two bullets struck Nicholson in the head. He was dead before he hit the floor.

Up in the conference room, Cairns and Hansen were down on their knees, trying to comfort Smith, when they heard a slight gurgling sound. It had come from Goertz. Cairns motioned for Hansen to check on Goertz. But as Hansen rose, he looked up and saw Lu.

Still brandishing the pistol, Lu slowly walked in. Now full of nervous energy, he began pacing this way and that. Hansen knew that Lu had come to finish off Smith: Lu had the look of a sick kid about to torture a frog.

"Lu Gang, don't!" Hansen begged.

"Get out," Lu ordered Hansen and Cairns. But his eyes were on Smith.

Hansen and Cairns didn't argue with the berserk gunman.

"He was calm and methodical," Cairns recalled. "He knew what he was doing. He didn't seem emotional at all.....I suppose I was still in shock. Perhaps I could have struggled, but I have no training, and three children."

Cairns and Hansen left, quickly ducking into room 306, where they joined Talbert. The men locked the door and turned off the lights.

Bob Smith knew he was about to be executed, but he was utterly helpless. Lu approached until he was only a half step away. From point-blank range, he pumped two slugs into Smith's head.

But Lu still wasn't done. He walked back around the conference table, to where his first two victims were slumped in their chairs, and pumped two more rounds into Goertz—one in the head, the other in the neck. Then he shot Shan again—also in the head.

Even then, the carnage wasn't over—because Lu had yet other scores to settle. Quickly he made his way back down the same stairwell and went outside, heading west on Jefferson Street. He walked deliberately toward Jessup Hall, the university's administration building—one of five imposing buildings that anchor the Pentacrest. The day was already turning dark, and there were few pedestrians or motorists out in the wet sleet and snow that were whipped by a bracing wind. Against the red light, Lu hardly bothered to look up as he crossed the normally busy four-lane Dubuque Street.

Only a block away from the Pentacrest now, he strode past the biology building. As he walked by the Congregational United Church of Christ, the Pentacrest came into view.

Behind him, Lu heard the distant wail of sirens as police and paramedics raced toward Van Allen Hall. One police cruiser even passed him going the other way on Jefferson, its lights flashing.

Now Lu was almost to the Pentacrest. All he had to do was cross Clinton Street. He was so focused on his next attack that he stepped into the roadway without looking—and was nearly struck by a passing automobile. But he kept right on going. Nothing could stop him now.

* * *

Within minutes of the first shots, frantic calls from Van Allen Hall inundated the Iowa City Police Department. But law-enforcement officials had a difficult time discerning what had taken place. Typical was the call they received from Cairns, who simply blurted out "There are two dead men in there!"

For the Iowa City Police Department, the calls could not have come at a worst time. About half of its fifty-five-member force was still in Cedar Rapids, at the shooting range for their annual firearms qualifications. And the department was in the midst of a major overhaul of its communications center. Normally, all 911 calls are automatically recorded. But the computers were temporarily disconnected because of the remodeling work. And so the dispatcher—new to the job—had to manually record each call, as well as log in the radio traffic. "It was a very confusing situation," recalled Capt. Donald H. Strand, who was in charge of the department's emergency communications.

Sgt. Craig Lihs was the watch supervisor that afternoon, in charge of the 3 P.M.–11 P.M. shift. He was alone in a "cruiser," fretting about the deteriorating road conditions, when the call went out to all patrol cars: There's been a shooting at Van Allen Hall.

Impossible, Lihs thought. This is Iowa City, Iowa. People don't get shot here. But he was just four blocks away, so he drove to the building. Several other cruisers were already there.

When Lihs reached the third-floor conference room and saw the blood and the bodies, his first thought was that there had been some awful laboratory accident. This was, after all, a science building. But the pungent smell of gunpowder was a sure giveaway. Then Lihs saw the bullet holes in the foreheads of Christoph Goertz and Shan Linhua.

"Oh, my God!" Lihs muttered to himself. And he pulled out his service revolver.

Just then, Lihs's walkie-talkie cackled with a new and

chilling message: There was another dead man—on the second floor. Before he could react, there came yet another report: People have been shot in Jessup Hall. "What the hell's going on?" Lihs wondered. And that report sent a chill up his spine for yet another reason: His wife worked in Jessup Hall.

Lihs quickly left others in charge at Van Allen Hall and sped to the Pentacrest.

"In here! In here!" people shouted as Lihs ran into the north entrance of the administration building, bounding up the steps two at a time. Other officers arrived at the same time, entering from the south entrance.

At the top of the steps, just inside the Office of Academic Affairs, two women lay on the floor. They also had been shot, and clearly were grievously wounded. No one seemed to know where the gunman was. Or even whether there was more than one.

* * *

Lu also had entered Jessup Hall by the north entrance, and gone directly to the Office of Academic Affairs. He was gunning for Anne Cleary. But the first person he encountered inside room 111 was Miya Rodolfo-Sioson, a Philippine-born coed who was finishing her second week on the job as a temporary receptionist. "He seemed very nervous, and asked to see Anne Cleary," Miya recalled. She asked Lu for his name, and then excused herself, stepping around him to go back to Cleary's office. "Oh, I don't want to see him," Cleary told Miya.

Just that morning, Cleary had talked about the querulous Lu with Les Sims, telling the dean of the Graduate College that she had concluded that Lu's allegations against Nicholson were groundless. She told Sims she intended soon to convey that to Lu, and the dean agreed it would be a good idea. But on that Friday afternoon, Cleary was in no mood to see Lu. Her niece from Chicago, Jean, was in town visiting, and she was eager to wrap up her work in time to take Jean out to dinner with some friends.

When Rodolfo-Sioson returned, Lu refused to take no for an answer. He created such a commotion that Cleary soon came out to the front reception area. Their conversation began in a civilized—even hushed—tone. But both quickly became agitated, Lu appearing especially hostile.

Miya, also eager to start her weekend, was intent on finishing her word-processing chores. But the strident voices became impossible to ignore. The next thing she heard was a loud bang. She had never heard the sound of a gunshot before, and didn't recognize it as such. But, as she looked in its direction, she saw Cleary fall to the floor.

Wordlessly, Lu wheeled and pointed the gun in Rodolfo-Sioson's face—right between her eyes. In the same nanosecond that he fingered the trigger, she started to stand. And that saved her life. The bullet, instead of penetrating her forehead, entered her mouth. And then she, too, fell.

*   *   *

In Van Allen Hall, pandemonium reigned on the second and third floors. Faculty members, students, and staffers roamed the corridors—some weeping, others wailing. Many talked in loud and excited tones, spreading the horrifying news. More and more people began congregating in the hallways.

Into this chaos stormed heavily armed police officers, some with shotguns at the ready. They raced up and down the corridors, ordering everyone to return to their offices and classrooms, to turn off the lights, to lie low, and—above all to lock the doors.

The police had to conduct a room-by-room search. They had no idea where the killer was. In fact, they woman had described the killer as a young Asian wearing a brown jacket. Great, Sergeant Lihs thought—that fit the description of nearly half the people in Van Allen Hall. Indeed, the officers had already frisked one frightened Asian student before sending him on his way. Another witness excitedly told police that she had seen a man with a rifle. If so, Lihs realized, there were at least two killers still on the prowl.

On the seventh floor, James Van Allen, the seventy-year-old chairman emeritus, had been sitting at his desk when Bruce Randall, a postdoctoral student, burst into his office, breathless. "Close your door, Van! Somebody's shooting down on the third floor!" Randall yelled before dashing down the hall to spread the alarm further. Looking out the window, Van Allen soon saw police cars and ambulances skidding to a halt down below. A half hour later, Evelyn Robinson, his longtime aide, gently tapped on his door: all clear.

Van Allen quickly went down to the department's second-floor office, where he ran into Gerald Payne, one of the professors. "Dwight and Chris and Bob have all been shot dead," Payne told him. Stunned, Van Allen got in his car and drove home. Abigail, his wife, had not yet heard of the shootings—but instantly she knew something was wrong. Her husband's face was ashen.

*   *   *

W. J. Winkelhake, Iowa City's police chief, was at his desk when the first 911 calls were logged in by hand. "There's been a shooting at the university," a secretary advised him.

Winkelhake decided to go to the scene, just a few blocks away. But as he was pulling in to Van Allen Hall, there came the reports of more shootings—this time at Jessup Hall. And Winkelhake's wife, Kathleen, worked there.

The chief immediately raced over to Jessup, arriving

at the same time as several other police officers and teams of paramedics. "Upstairs!" someone inside yelled as the policemen charged into the administration building, their guns drawn.

Leading the charge, Winkelhake ran past the Academic Affairs Office on the first landing, where he caught a glimpse of people tending to Cleary and Rodolfo-Sioson. He continued up to the second floor, where he saw Kathleen. Relieved, the chief told her, "Stay in there and lock the door."

She nodded, but told her husband: "I just heard a gunshot down the hall," pointing toward the other end of the second-floor corridor. Winkelhake trusted her judgment: She had spent time at the range and knew the difference between a gunshot and a firecracker—or the sound of a car engine backfiring.

So the shootings were *not* over. His adrenaline surging, Winkelhake and two of his men cautiously worked their way down the wide corridor, checking room after room while covering one another, unsure of whether they would encounter another victim or confront the killer.

The corridor now was eerily silent except for the footsteps of the officers, echoing off the gray metal wall lockers that lined both walls. Behind some of the doors, in darkened classrooms, the officers found students cowering under their desks.

Finally, Winkelhake reached the other end of the corridor, where the hall splits off perpendicularly, making way for a square classroom around which the corridor detours before meeting up again on the other side. It was there—inside the island classroom—that the search ended.

*   *   *

After Lu shot Rodolfo-Sioson, he immediately stalked out of the Academic Affairs Office and began striding down the first-floor corridor toward the office of the university's president. Perhaps he intended to kill Hunter Rawlings next. But time had just about ran out.

As he reached Rawlings's suite of offices at the far end of Jessup Hall, Lu heard one vehicle after another pulling up outside, their sirens wailing. But instead of going in, Lu abruptly turned left and went up the south stairwell. As he climbed the steps, once again reloading his Taurus, Lu passed a bronze bust of Walter Albert Jessup, the university's president from 1916 to 1934. But Lu had no time to soak up any history. He was too busy making it.

On the second floor, he made a hard left. Room 203 was just across a narrow hallway from the Affirmative Action Office, to which Lu had first taken his complaint about Nicholson. But if Lu had intended to exact revenge on that office, there was just no more time: He could hear the sounds of police officers storming the building. They were closing in.

Although room 203 had no windows, each of the two doors had a see-through panel. Grateful to find the room unoccupied, Lu stepped in. Calmly, he took off his brown jacket and draped it neatly over the back of a chair, the unused .22-caliber pistol still in one pocket. Then he sat down in another chair, still clutching the .38-caliber weapon in his right hand.

As he heard footsteps of the policemen coming down the hallway, Lu put the gun to his right temple and took up the slack on the trigger. The bullet ripped through his skull and landed on the linoleum tile floor seven feet away, smeared with brain matter. Lu pitched forward, fell to the floor, and rolled over.

*   *   *

Winkelhake and his men burst into room 203 with their guns drawn. The acrid smell of fresh gunpowder hung heavy in the small, oppressive classroom. Lu lay on his back in a pool of thickening blood, his right hand still clutching the sidearm. His chest heaved and his limbs quivered. The end was coming fast, if not already at hand.

Winkelhake, however, was not one to take chances: "Cuff him," he ordered.

FIFTEEN

Ripples

Even after they had found Lu Gang, the police still couldn't be absolutely certain that there wasn't another killer on the loose. At least two people in Van Allen Hall claimed to have seen a second gunman—one carrying a rifle or shotgun.

It took the officers nearly an hour to establish that the witnesses somehow had mistaken a police officer for a gunman. And the process of searching Van Allen Hall and Jessup Hall room by room was severely hampered by a surprisingly large number of offices that officials couldn't open because the locks had been changed without authorization.

The frantic chaos began to subside when Adam Usadi stepped forward. A twenty-four-year-old physics graduate student from New York who had met Lu through a room-mate-matching service just two months earlier, Usadi had been living with Lu in the Jefferson Street apartment. When he heard about the shootings at Van Allen Hall, Usadi had a chilling premonition that Lu might have been involved. He rushed to Van Allen Hall. Police then took him to Jessup Hall—where he sadly identified Lu's body.

News of the shootings spread instantaneously. Within

minutes a local radio reporter was broadcasting live from the campus as he dashed back and forth between Van Allen and Jessup halls.

Another person who came forth with vital information was Bill Gold, who had waited on Lu only an hour earlier at Pak Mail. Acting on Gold's information, authorities were able to intercept, and confiscate as potential evidence, Lu's final letters and packages.

At Jessup Hall, university officials initially were clueless about Lu's motives. In the Office of Academic Affairs, paramedics frantically worked over Anne Cleary and Miya Rodolfo-Sioson. Several women in that office were hysterical. Others milled about in a daze, weeping. "People were a mess. Everybody was in shock, zombie-like," recalled Julia Mears, a university lawyer who worked in Jessup Hall. "People were just standing around, not knowing what to do and yet not wanting to go home."

At the other end of Jessup's first-floor hallway, inside the office suite of president Hunter Rawlings, the secretaries were still hiding under their desks, cowering in fear. One of them, Anna K. Huntzinger, the president's assistant, was on the telephone with Rawlings. He was in a hotel room in Columbus, Ohio, preparing to attend a University of Iowa alumni fund-raising reception, to be followed the next day by the Ohio State–Iowa football game. Rawlings had been on the telephone with someone else, but an operator cut in, saying he had an emergency call.

Huntzinger told Rawlings of the shootings, adding that—even as they were speaking—the gunman was still roaming Jessup Hall.

"It was very, very frightening," Rawlings recalled. But there was nothing he could do.

"Have you called the police?"

"Yes, we have. They're on the way."

"Are your doors locked?"

"Yes. Everyone's crouched under their desks."

"Be careful. Call me back as soon as you can."

Moments later, Huntzinger did the latter, to tell Rawlings that the gunman had committed suicide—in a classroom directly above their office. However, because of the ferocious snowstorm in Iowa City, Rawlings was unable to return until the next day.

It wasn't until Les Sims, dean of the Graduate College, arrived at Jessup Hall that university officials had an explanation for the shootings. Minutes before the shootings began, Sims had gone to the barber shop for a quick Friday afternoon haircut. When he returned, a secretary told him about the massacre. Sims then made his way across the street to Jessup Hall, telling his stunned university colleagues about Lu and his grievances. One of the first things Sims saw upon entering Jessup Hall was a seriously wounded Anne Cleary, with whom he had spoken only hours earlier—about Lu.

Further illumination of Lu's actions came as officials opened his briefcase, which he had deliberately left behind in the Van Allen Hall conference room. In it was Lu's public statement.

A new sense of urgency arose after authorities came across Lu's letter to his sister. It was written in Chinese. "There was this fear of: 'What else had he done?'" Mears recalled. What if Lu had accomplices, or he had planted bombs that were still ticking? Perhaps the letter contained some reference to such. Hastily, officials located a university Chinese scholar, W. South Coblin, and had him translate the letter to Huimin. Only after Coblin had completed the translation did university officials breath a collective sigh of relief: The massacre was over, and life—though for some forever changed—could go on.

* * *

Like Hunter Rawlings, Peter Nathan—the university's second-ranking official—also was out of town on the afternoon of the killings. He was in Chicago, enroute home from Costa Rica, where he had attended an international conference on rural health care. Nathan was at a departure gate at O'Hare International Airport when other Iowa City–bound passengers approached him to ask for details of the shootings.

Nathan was stunned. He hadn't heard yet. He dashed to a pay phone, but all circuits to Iowa City were busy. News of the deaths and injuries had been broadcast within ten minutes of their occurrence by both CNN and National Public Radio. As a result, concerned parents, relatives, and friends began calling from all over the country, quickly overwhelming the telephone system. During a normal hour, Iowa City records an average of 12,000 phone calls. But after news of the incident began circulating, the number of calls tripled, peaking at 11,000 between 5 P.M. and 5:15 P.M.

It might have eased the avalanche of calls had authorities been able, early on, to release the names of the victims. But until officials could reach the next of kin of each victim, their hands were tied. Thus most out-of-town callers, even after identifying themselves and the person they were calling about, were simply told that the person in question was unharmed. Some callers, however, also were told that the dead students were foreigners.

At Jessup Hall, despite the absences of Rawlings and Nathan, university officials quickly got organized to deal with the catastrophe. They already had in place an "administrative liaison group," a committee of six senior officials that, since the 1960s, had planned for and responded to student demonstrations, tornadoes, floods, and even controversial speakers on campus. The group hastily set up a command center in Rawlings's conference room, under the direction of Phillip E. Jones, associate vice president and dean of students.

Within minutes of the shootings, the campus was swarming with city police officers, members of the unarmed campus security force, Johnson County sheriff's deputies, state highway patrolmen, fire and rescue teams, and representatives of the county coroner's office. Their work had to be coordinated. The governor, the attorney general, and the state Board of Regents—all had to be quickly notified. The Chinese government had to be informed. University buildings had to be secured and the evidence preserved. Counselors had to be summoned to both Jessup and Van Allen halls, to deal with the distraught.

A news media center had to be set up; the demand for information was overwhelming. "I've dealt with the news media, but I've never seen so many reporters," recalled Pat White, the Johnson County prosecutor. He learned of the shootings from a radio report while driving home—very slowly, in the blinding snowstorm—from Des Moines, where he had chaired a meeting on compensation for crime victims. Tuning in to KXIC, an Iowa City station, White recognized the familiar voice of reporter Roy Justis, who was clearly panting on the air. White at first thought Justis was doing a feature story on jogging. In fact, Justis was reporting, live, while dashing from one crime scene to the other.

The job of dealing with the press fell to Ann Rhodes, vice president for university relations. She had taken the day off and had just returned home after an outing with her six-year-old daughter when Rawlings's office called with news of the massacre. It normally took Rhodes about ten minutes to drive to her office, but she got there in five, despite the treacherous road conditions. She knew it was urgent to get out as much information, and as accurately, as possible.

But the most important, and most delicate, job of all fell on those dispatched to visit the murder victims' loved ones.

* * *

Ulrike Goertz and Greg Smith, the wives of Christoph Goertz and Bob Smith, were together when Les Sims, Pat White, and a counselor arrived at the Goertzes' home on North Linn Street.

The women already knew. So did Goertz's elderly mother, who was in town visiting. Someone from the physics department had called. Still, they looked at the three men questioningly upon their arrival. "They knew. But they didn't want to know," Sims recalled.

Ulrike Goertz became furious when told that she could not go to Van Allen Hall just then to see her husband's body. She insisted that she had a right to do so. "My property" were the wrenching words she used. The woman almost had to be physically restrained. Later she was further incited when, in the unavoidable chaos of the moment, no one realized until too late that Chris Goertz had wanted to donate a kidney to a diabetic brother living in Germany.

In Tulsa, Jane Nicholson got the shattering news by phone from Gerald Payne, just as she returned from a trip to the grocery store. Payne found the news so difficult to deliver that he couldn't bring himself to tell her—until later that night—that many others had also been murdered.

It fell to officials of the Chinese consulate, summoned from Chicago, to alert the family of Lu Gang. They eventually reached Lu's brother-in-law via a fax machine.

On Morningside Drive in Iowa City, Erik Nilausen and Cheryl Tugwell were home eating pizza and watching the news on television with a guest, a young Russian student from the university. At the first, sketchy reports, Tugwell called her parents in North Carolina. "But don't worry. We're not involved," she assured them.

Nilausen and Tugwell watched Ann Rhodes say at the TV news conference that she could not yet release the names of the victims, since family members were still in the process of being notified. But when Rhodes said that the killer had been "apparently distraught" over the awarding of the Spriesterbach Award to a competitor, Nilausen suddenly knew. He slammed his fist against the tabletop and stormed out of the room.

Puzzled, Tugwell ran after Nilausen, demanding an explanation. Only a week earlier, he said, he had run into Shan Linhua near the campus during the lunch hour, and Shan had told him about winning the award—promising to invite Nilausen and Tugwell to the awards reception. Tugwell felt a chill run up her spine, but urged her husband not to jump to conclusions.

Tugwell then quickly called Yang Yiling. "Have you talked to Shan?" she asked nonchalantly. "Do you know where he is?"

"No, but we're waiting for him to call, to pick us up for dinner," Yang replied—referring to herself and her father, who had arrived in Illinois just that week to become a visiting research scientist at the University of Illinois in Champaign-Urbana. Yang and Shan had driven down to help him get settled; and friends there had urged them to stay and party through the weekend—but Shan had politely declined: He had an important physics seminar back in Iowa City on Friday afternoon. Then he and Yang had brought her father back to Iowa for the weekend.

"I'll get off the phone so Shan can get through," Tugwell said, her own fears deepening.

Despite the terrible road conditions, she and Nilausen jumped in their car and drove to Yang's place at the Parklawn Apartments across the river. As soon as they arrived, they knew the awful truth. A number of grim-faced university officials were already there, and so were many of Shan's and Yang's friends, looking distraught and in shock.

"How do you know?" Yang shrilly demanded of Gary Althen of the Office of International Education and

Services. She didn't realize that he had been dispatched as the official university representative bearing the tragic news.

Turning to the Reverend Jason Chen, Yang said—beseechingly, as if hoping the minister could confirm her words: "He's okay. He's going to be home any minute now. They all say he's dead. But I don't believe it!"

"No, Yiling. They're right, and that's the reason I'm here," Chen told her.

Now on the verge of hysteria, Yang asked him: "How could God have allowed this to happen?"

"Yeah, how does your church explain *this*?" Yang's greatly hurt father tearfully inquired.

Tugwell and Nilausen did what they could to comfort Yang and her father and then went home, leaving them with a host of her friends and neighbors.

The next morning, Tugwell began calling around to help Yang make funeral arrangements for Shan. Then she and Nilausen accompanied Yang to the morgue to identify the body. "At that point, we were literally holding her up," Tugwell recalled.

Yang approached Shan's body tentatively, as if still unwilling to believe that he was dead. Slowly she reached out a hand and gently laid it on top of his head—and then began caressing him. When she reached the back of his head, blood suddenly seeped out of a rear bullet wound, onto her now trembling fingers.

Another shattering moment for Yang came two days later, when she went to the funeral home to pick out a casket. "We walked in and there was this room full of caskets," Tugwell recalled. "I can't do this," Yang wailed—and collapsed to the floor. But when her friends and father appeared ready to step in and select a casket, Yang quickly pulled herself together—and again took charge.

✻   ✻   ✻

Like Shan, Cleary also had a good potential reason to be out of town on that terrible Friday afternoon. One of her three brothers, Michael, who lived in Brussels, was in New York City on business. And so was another brother, Paul, who lived in Boston. Her third brother, Frank, lived in West Redding, Connecticut. It was a perfect opportunity for a sibling reunion that weekend. But Anne didn't think she could get away—there was too much work to do.

Lu Gang shot Cleary in the left nostril. When the paramedics reached Jessup Hall, she still had a pulse—though a weak one. They rushed her to the hospital, but nothing could be done for her, and she was put on life support. That night, a number of Cleary's friends rushed to be with her—including Janet White. At her bedside, White prayed, and told Cleary how much she was loved. A tear rolled down Cleary's cheek.

The next day, all three of Anne's brothers arrived. Cleary had irreversible brain damage and was being kept alive only by artificial means. Shortly after noon the brothers, along with two of their wives and Peg Clifford, Anne Cleary's closest friend, met with the medical team and made the heart-rending decision. "It was an unambiguous issue," said Paul Cleary. "There was no question in our minds." A little after 1:30 P.M. that day, Anne Cleary was disconnected from her life-support system. She died peacefully a few minutes later.

"Anne had this capacity to make you feel special," said Elizabeth M. Altmaier, a friend and protégé of Cleary's who now is the university's associate vice president of academic affairs. "And it wasn't until her funeral that you discovered that she was so special to many, many people."

Except Lu Gang.

SIXTEEN

Amazing Grace

More than five hundred people came to Anne Cleary's funeral. In death, as in life, she exerted a strong influence on the community that she so loved.

Almost immediately after the shootings, some spoke darkly about foreign students, with the Chinese singled out for special criticism. Such rumblings alarmed both university and city officials, who were still trying to figure out how to help everyone—themselves included—to cope with the shattering events.

In that tense, uncertain time, on the frigid and windy day that Anne Cleary was laid to rest in Iowa City's St. Joseph's Cemetery, the three Cleary brothers jointly released a copy of a letter they had sent to Lu Gang's family in China. "It was one of the most important things that happened afterward," recalled Hunter Rawlings.

The Clearys publicly forgave Lu, and said their sister would have demanded nothing less. "We asked ourselves: 'How would Anne have liked us to behave?' If there were any backlash against foreign students or the students from China, she would roll over in her grave," Paul Cleary said.

The brothers' letter was addressed "To the family of Lu Gang." Here is what it said:

> We have just lived through an immense and sudden tragedy. We have lost our sister in the prime of her life. We are very proud of her. She made an impact, and was loved and respected by everyone she touched—her family, neighbors, their children, colleagues in the academic environment, her students, and friends and relatives throughout the world.
>
> As our family came together here in Iowa from distant places, we shared our grief with so many of her friends, but we also shared the wonderful memories of Anne and the gift she was to all of us.
>
> As we gathered in grief and fond memories, our thoughts and prayers also went out to you, the family of Lu Gang, as we know how you also must be grieving at this time. You also must be sharing in the shock and sorrow of this weekend.
>
> Anne believed in love and forgiveness, and we would like to reach out to you in your grief, and share our prayers and love with you at this very difficult time. During this time of pain, Anne would want our hearts to be filled with compassion, generosity and love. We all know that the only family which feels more grief than us at this time is your family, and we want you to know that we are with you in this sorrow.
>
> Together, we all can gain strength and support from this. Anne would want it that way.

"Their reaching out to the Chinese community was crucial in the healing process," said Maile-Gene Sagen and Barbara A. Schwartz of the office of the university ombudsperson. The brothers' letter was read during Cleary's funeral mass, held at St. Patrick's Catholic Church. There, a small table next to her closed casket held a photograph of a smiling Anne Cleary, rosaries to be given to her eight nephews and nieces, and crosses for her three brothers. There were also three roses in a vase—one each from Betsy, Rachel, and Nathan White, the neighborhood children who had received countless roses from Cleary over the years to mark milestones in their young lives. Later the flowers were placed atop Cleary's casket as it was lowered into the earth.

After the service, Paul Cleary held a press conference and elaborated on the family's feelings about forgiveness. "Anne would raise her head up and chide us if we, or anyone in the community, or anyone around the country used this as an opportunity to generate anger," he said. "Perhaps the only family that feels more grief than us is Lu Gang's family, and we want them to understand that we are with them in this sorrow and we support them. We pray for them and we love them and we want everyone in the country to know that this should not be a divisive episode. This should be an episode where we build on the achievements of a remarkable, sensitive, caring woman."

✻   ✻   ✻

The bullet that struck Miya Rodolfo-Sioson in the mouth lodged in her fifth vertebra, damaging her spinal cord. It left her paralyzed from the neck down. But—even while in a hospital bed—the resilient twenty-three-year-old almost immediately began a healing process that inspired the entire community.

Initially, Rodolfo-Sioson's will to live wavered, and her condition even posed legal questions about removing the ventilator that was helping her breathe. "It was hard not to be depressed," she later said—recalling her respiratory failures, the insomnia, the boredom, the despair. But then she snapped out of it, and her indomitable spirit took hold.

She vowed to spend the rest of her life working for human rights and justice—especially in Latin America.

Rodolfo-Sioson already had something of a profile on campus because of her activism in promoting peace and human rights. As a senior, she was a member of the honor society. Working her way through school, she had held a variety of jobs, including taking care of a paraplegic student. But the patient, injured in a wrestling accident, was moody and erratic in terms of when he required her services. Since Rodolfo-Sioson found herself in need of steadier, more predictable income, she signed up with Manpower Temporary Services—and the agency sent her to the university's Office of Academic Affairs. November first, the day she was shot, was only her tenth day on the job.

Rodolfo-Sioson's parents were from the Philippines, and she had been born in Manila. Her father, a U.S.-educated mathematician, brought the family to America when he got a teaching job at Iowa State University, in Ames. But not long after that he died—leaving his wife, Sonia (who had earned a Ph.D. in physiology and pharmacology) to raise Miya and her three older brothers. The family lived in Dhahran, Saudi Arabia, for four years before returning to Iowa in 1982.

At the time of the shooting, Rodolfo-Sioson and her family had been planning a trip back to the Philippines in December, their first return in fifteen years. A month earlier, Rodolfo-Sioson had become a United States citizen.

The young woman's struggle captured the hearts of most everyone in the community. Hunter Rawlings ordered university administrators to see that her medical bills were taken care of. Separately, her friends began an ambitious fund-raising drive, with donation cans being passed around at athletic events. Many businesses also joined in, holding charity drives on their own.

Rodolfo-Sioson would need a lifetime of physical rehabilitation and around-the-clock care. In that first year a quarter-million dollars was raised, allowing her to spend more than three months at the famed Rehabilitation Institute in Chicago for physical therapy—and, later, to buy a specially equipped van.

"It seemed like everybody came out to volunteer and help," a grateful Rodolfo-Sioson said. "I never thought Iowa City had a really strong sense of community before." The outpouring of support from that community was in fact the major reason that she decided to remain in Iowa City. "There's really nothing to be angry at," she added. "You wish he were still alive so you could yell at him: 'Why me?' But the guy's dead. So, in some ways, it's easier this way."

Rodolfo-Sioson spends much of her time in a specially equipped house a few blocks from the campus, where she has a mechanized wheelchair and a personal computer controlled by a "magic wand" minikeyboard. In her sun-drenched corner bedroom is a black box that recognizes human voices, allowing her to command it to turn on and off a lamp, the television set, and the alarm clock. Her biggest frustration, she has said, is the slow pace with which she is learning to adapt to her "new surroundings."

"Miya is an inspiration," Rawlings said on NBC's *Today Show* on the first anniversary of the shootings. "She seems so remarkably free from anger from this incident, so pointed toward the rest of her life." But it was Rodolfo-Sioson herself who said it best:

"I have come to realize that my problems are really no worse than anyone else's—only more visible because they are physical and well-advertised through the media. I believe, or I like to believe, that I would be able to forgive Lu Gang if he were alive. Reflecting on the shooting, I can only attempt to understand the tremendous alienation and pain he must have experienced to have committed such horrible crimes. Through this experience, I have come to realize how lucky I am to be given a second lease on life and to be surrounded by such caring people in my circle of friends and family and in the community at large.

"By snapping us out of our daily routine, the shooting refocused our priorities and provided us the opportunity to communicate feelings rarely expressed before the tragedy. If there is one important lesson to be gained from such a violent act, it is the triumph of love, friendship, and forgiveness."

The sole survivor of the shootings, Miya Rodolfo-Sioson was also Lu's only random victim. Why he shot her will never be known.

Epilogue

The devastated physics department struggled valiantly to go on. With the encouragement of the four widows, its annual Christmas party was held as previously scheduled, barely a month after the murders. More than a hundred people attended the event, which was held in a small ballroom at the Student Union. Though hardly the festive affair that it normally was, "It was a positive thing," said Karen Phelps, who made most of the arrangements for the party. "We needed to do something normal. It was a step forward."

The department's theoretical space physics research group was virtually wiped out, and it took nearly two full years to find permanent replacements for the slain professors. But that wasn't the end of adversity: The huge NASA grant awarded to the Goertz-led group wasn't renewed after it expired at the end of 1993. "NASA gave us some close-out money, that was all," said Gerald L. Payne, who succeeded Nicholson as chairman of the department of physics and astronomy.

"A fair number of projects just kind of withered—there was nobody there to continue them," lamented John Lyons. "Chris Goertz had a very fertile intellect. He could toss out ideas faster than anybody could follow them up. That sort of person is sorely missed."

For more than a year, Van Allen took over the editorship of the *Journal of Geophysical Research*, until a

186

permanent editor to replace Goertz was found and the publication moved to the University of Michigan.

In Washington, big science projects, widely blamed for draining funds from individual researchers, ran into serious congressional opposition in 1993, and one (the $11 billion superconducting supercollider in Texas) was killed outright. The $30 billion space station was now to be built as a joint United States–Russia venture.

In Congress, Rep. George E. Brown Jr. also began making some headway in his crusade against direct appropriations for science and technology projects. Such congressional earmarking reached a record $763 million in 1993, but, under Brown's prodding, the House of Representatives reversed itself and voted to subject more than $230 million in previously appropriated "pork" to an open process of competitive bidding and review.

It remains to be seen whether individual researchers get any of the savings that might accrue from cutting back on mega-science projects or from a more open, competitive bidding process. Meanwhile, job prospects for scientists were as gloomy in 1994 as in preceding years. "Things are just in a holding pattern," said one science official.

＊　＊　＊

The Iowa killings led to the creation of the November First Coalition, a grassroots organization formed by Iowa City gun-control advocates. The widows of those killed on November 1, 1991, gave the movement a boost by publicly calling for much stricter firearm regulations.

"I've heard handgun advocates say that if someone is determined to kill somebody, they will," Greg Smith said shortly after the killings. "Bob was moving to escape after the first two shots. Lu Gang...then went downstairs...and came back upstairs to finish the job. There were other people in the room. If Lu Gang had had a knife, someone would have hit him with a chair or pushed the table at him.

But there was no way they could fight against a handgun. My husband, my child's father, should be alive today. With things the way they are in this country, this could happen to anybody, anytime. It could happen to your family. Handguns make it too easy to kill. Handguns do kill people and that's the issue."

Jane Nicholson added: "Six people died and a young woman is paralyzed for life because a lethal weapon was too readily acquired by an individual in stress. We must rediscover and create ways to be empathetic toward each other no matter what the nature or scale of our human dilemmas."

In November 1993, Congress finally passed the Brady Bill, which imposes a five-day waiting period before a person may purchase a handgun, giving authorities time to conduct a background check on the prospective buyer. In the preceding two years, firearms had killed 60,000 Americans—more than the number of U.S. soldiers killed in the Vietnam War.

With public safety a growing concern, fueled by a rash of mass murders throughout the country, within days after President Clinton signed the Brady Bill there were signs that even stricter controls over the possession of weapons might well be in the offing. One special target was the semiautomatic assault weapon—of the sort used by Wayne Lo, an honors student who killed two people and injured four others at an exclusive college in Massachusetts only a year after the Iowa murders. Such a ban became law in late 1994.

The University of Iowa killings also underscored the increasing dangers of the workplace. According to the American Management Association, nearly a quarter of 311 companies it surveyed said that at least one of their workers had been attacked or killed on the job since 1990. And in 1993 alone, more than 1,000 people were murdered on the job, according to the U.S. Labor Department.

Crime on college campuses also is rising. According to the *Chronicle of Higher Education* in 1993, the first annual crime statistics submitted by more than 2,400 schools turned up 30 murders, almost 1,000 rapes, more than 1,800 robberies, 32,000 burglaries, and nearly 9,000 car thefts. The crime wave has actually prompted some colleges and universities to tout their special security measures as a selling point.

* * *

The four widows benefited from the fact that Iowa has among the most generous workers' compensation programs in the nation. For life, unless they remarry, Ulrike Goertz, Jane Nicholson, and Greg Smith each will receive about $38,000 a year, and Yang Yiling about $19,000. The amounts are based on the salaries their husbands made at the time of their deaths. The university also provided assistance to the families in numerous ways, including an extra paycheck, full retirement benefits, life insurance, and burial fees. What little there was of Lu Gang's estate, including his car, was disposed of, under court supervision, by Alan Bohanan, a local attorney. The several thousand dollars ended up going to Miya Rodolfo-Sioson for her medical bills.

Two weeks after the killings, Jane Nicholson returned to the University of Tulsa, resuming her life in Oklahoma as a professor. "In Tulsa, only a few people knew. But in Iowa City, everybody knew. Even strangers," she recalled.

Nicholson said she never knew what pain could be until her husband was murdered. At times she was not sure she wanted to go on living. "I was stricken, just stricken," she said. Constantly, she "danced" with her grief. There was no time or place where it was not present. Nicholson later realized that "It was too painful for friends and family to see me in that kind of pain," and so she began to seek professional counseling. "I'd never spent so much time taking care of myself," she recalled, laughing with a dash of self-consciousness. "But I grew enormously. In many ways, I feel like I've been transformed—for example, I'm much more open than ever to new kinds of experiences."

Nicholson returned to Iowa City six months after her husband's death, to take part in the ceremonial tree planting outside Van Allen Hall. "That was the hardest time for me. I was very, very blue during the ceremony. It was real depressing. That was when I hit the low point," she said. On the first anniversary of the murders, she returned once more to take part in the public remembrances. "I needed to be there to represent Dwight, and it was also a part of my own healing process," she said. After that day, she decided that she could "stop being the public figure."

Nicholson also decided then that she could stop being the widow. At the end of the day, she removed her wedding ring. Back in Tulsa, she began thinking vaguely about getting out of academia—not because of fear of "being blown apart," but because of her own growing disenchant-ment with the hierarchical nature of academic life. She also wanted to do more writing—perhaps exploring the grieving process—and to become more involved in the gun-control movement.

Yang Yiling began working toward a U.S. degree in electrical engineering. Uncomfortable with the idea of somehow profiting from her husband's murder, she sent most of the money that came pouring in after his death to his family in China.

Greg Smith and Ulrike Goertz kept much lower public profiles. Smith, a teaching assistant in the art department, didn't even appear with the widows when they held a press conference shortly after the killings to call for gun control. Goertz, a teaching assistant in nutrition and public health, continued to cling to her conviction that the university was partly to blame for what happened. More than a year after the killings, she said she thought that Lu Gang was *not* a madman. "What is it about the Chinese culture that makes it honorable to settle a dispute this way?" she snapped angrily. Said a friend: "She really wants to know who at the university slipped up, and when."

*   *   *

Lu Huimin, sister of the mass murderer, was the only other person to hold the university responsible for what happened. Her brother's rampage—and suicide—were "unbearable" to their parents, Huimin said. The university "bears a definite responsibility," she asserted. Her brother's "greatest hope" had been to be a scholar, Lu Huimin continued, adding: "He devoted his entire being to his studies, to the point that the placing of obstacles in the way of this endeavor would from his standpoint have been tantamount to destroying him." Thus, the university had "behaved unjustly" toward her brother. Had officials spent more time explaining things to her brother and investigating his complaints, Lu Huimin concluded, "This tragic incident could have been avoided."

*   *   *

After much soul-searching, university officials came to the conclusion that the killings had been, in the words of President Rawlings, "an idiosyncratic event."

"In a way, you don't ever recover fully from something like this. It's too traumatic. The sense of innocence—that's lost. Shattered. The loss of our faculty—you don't recover from that, either. It's too devastating.

"But there is a danger in overinterpreting," said Rawlings. "Certainly we've reviewed our handling of this incident. And we're satisfied that everyone here acted very honorably and carefully. Some have tried to make it out as the inevitable result of competition and pressure. That does exist—but it exists for everyone in graduate studies."

Added provost Peter Nathan, "There's no way, I'm quite

convinced, that we could have predicted this. There are thousands of graduate students who fit the same profile. Maybe some people in physics could have handled this a little bit differently and explained it to Lu Gang better. But I doubt if the outcome would have been different."

Such conviction is of course self-serving, to the extent that it exonerates the university from blame. And it misses the larger, more enduring question of how a dynamic, competitive university—any university—can better serve foreign graduate students, and indeed all its students.

In the aftermath of the November 1 killings, University of Iowa officials and the region's mental-health community did an extraordinary job of providing immediate, on-the-spot counseling for anyone who needed it—especially surviving family members and the many witnesses. But can, or should, that kind of commitment endure? Might not a voice of calm and reason have steered Lu toward a less destructive path?

And what can be done to better foster town-gown relations, so that more foreign students can be linked with committed, caring host families—people like Erik Nilausen and Cheryl Tugwell? In Iowa City, 250 to 300 host families already are serving in such a capacity, often taking on more than one student. But scores of other foreign students at any given time remain on a waiting list. "There's a real need for host families," said Gary Althen of the university's Office of International Education and Services. The informal student nationality organizations, he concluded, "do far more than we do."

And are procedures in place to guarantee the expeditious processing and monitoring of student grievances? Shouldn't mechanisms be developed to identify and assess the needs of troubled individuals? Shouldn't academic advisers strive to maintain closer ties with foreign students so the advisers would know, for instance, if one of their charges is so unhappy as to desire a change in majors?

"This institution doesn't do what it could to respond promptly and clearly to student grievances," Althen said. "It's easy to see how even an even-minded person can get distraught."

Finally, shouldn't the system ease up on graduate students? "I don't think the pressures are that strong on graduate students," said Gerald Payne. "Besides, what they encounter here is nothing compared to the pressures after they get out. I've been asked, but I don't know what to change if I could."

Van Allen put it this way: "We do conduct a very rigorous academic program in our department. And I think pressure would be one characterization of it. It's intended to be a rigorous, demanding program requiring high achievement."

Said University of Iowa physicist John Lyons: "The system generally gets tougher and more rigorous as one progresses. To some extent that's by design—to produce the best Ph.D. scientists. And I wouldn't say it's any tougher here than anywhere else. But on the other hand, you can reach the point where it's too much. And it's got to be different if this isn't your native culture, and I don't know to what extent those factors played in Lu Gang's perceptions. I've certainly run into people who made it a point to browbeat me—to see, you know, how I'd react. I told them to back off. But for someone who doesn't recognize the situation for what it is, cultural misunderstandings can easily come into play and he might react negatively."

* * *

The November 1 victims were memorialized in many different ways. Six months after the murders, a red oak sapling was planted outside Van Allen Hall. At its base was a rock containing a plaque bearing the names of the four slain physicists. Inside Van Allen Hall, a wall plaque was mounted outside the suite of rooms that served as Dwight Nicholson's office. And just off the Pentacrest, a new, tree-lined walkway was named for Anne Cleary. Scholarships also were started in honor of each victim.

But some thought the most appropriate remembrance of all was provided by Mother Nature. Exactly a week after the murders, the aurora borealis put on a spectacular and unprecedented display in the night skies over Iowa.

Bibliography

Althen, Gary. *American Ways: A Guide for Foreigners in the United States*. Intercultural Press, Yarmouth, Maine. 1988.

Bennett, Gordon A., and Ronald N. Montaperto. *Red Guard: The Political Biography of Dai Hsiao-Al*. Doubleday & Co., Garden City, NY. 1971.

Bergaust, Erik. *Wernher von Braun*. National Space Institute, Washington, D.C. 1976.

Boorstin, Daniel J. *The Americans: The Democratic Experience*. Random House, New York. 1974.

Bryan, C. D. B. *Friendly Fire*. G.P. Putnam's, New York. 1976.

Donovan, Katherine C. *Assisting Students and Scholars From the People's Republic of China*. Committee on Scholarly Communication With the People's Republic of China and the National Association for Foreign Student Affairs, Washington, D.C. 1981.

Fairbank, John K. *Chinabound: A Fifty-Year Memoir*. Harper & Row, New York. 1982.

——, Edwin O. Reischauer, and Albert M. Craig. *East Asia: Tradition and Transformation*. Houghton Mifflin, Boston. 1973.

Fairbank, Wilma. *America's Cultural Experiment in China: 1942–49*. Bureau of Educational and Cultural Affairs, State Department, Washington, D.C. 1976.

Halas, Christine D. *Guide to the James A. Van Allen Papers and Related Collections*. University of Iowa Archives, Iowa City, Iowa. 1993.

Herman, Robin. *Fusion: The Search for Endless Energy*. Cambridge University Press, Cambridge, England. 1990.

Manchester, William. *The Glory and the Dream: A Narrative History of America, 1932–1972*. Little, Brown Co., Boston. 1974.

Nee, Victor G., and Brett De Bary. *Longtime Californ': A Documentary Study of an American Chinatown*. Random House, New York. 1972.

Orleans, Leo A. *Chinese Students in America: Policies, Issues, and Numbers*. National Academy Press, Washington, D.C. 1988.

Reed, Linda A. *Education in the People's Republic of China and U.S.–China Educational Exchanges*. National Association for Foreign Student Affairs, Washington, D.C. 1988.

Sage, Leland L. *A History of Iowa*. Iowa State University Press, Ames, Iowa. 1974.

Schell, Orville, *To Get Rich Is Glorious: China in the '80s*. Random House, New York. 1984.

Trillin, Calvin. *Killings*. Viking Penguin, New York. 1984.

Index